STRATEGIES TO INCREASE SALES AND DRIVE REVENUE

Steve k. Bryant

Copyright

Copyright © 2024 by **Steve k. Bryant**

All rights reserved. No part of this publication may be reproduced, distributed, or transmitted in any form or by any means, including photocopying, recording, or other electronic or mechanical methods, without the prior written permission of the publisher, except in the case of brief quotations embodied in critical reviews and certain other noncommercial uses permitted by copyright law.

Contents

Introduction 7
    Importance of Sales and Cost Management in Business Growth 7
    The Role of Sales Teams in Driving Revenue 8
    Overview of 13 Strategies for Increasing Sales 9

Chapter One 17
Understanding Your Customers. 17
    Identifying the customer's needs, challenges, desires, and fears 17
    Methods to Gather Customer Insights 21

Chapter 2 29
Using the Sales Funnel Model 29
    Explanation of Sales Funnel Stages 29
    Strategies for Optimizing Each Stage 35
    Example of Effective Sales Funnel Implementation . 39

Chapter 3 43
Communicating with Customers Online 43
    Importance of Online Presence 43
    Platforms for Customer Interaction 45
    Best Practices in Online Communication 48

Case Studies for Successful Online Engagement 50

Chapter 4 55

Provides a Variety of Payment Options 55

    Understanding Customers' Payment Preferences 55

    Importance of Payment Options 55

    Different Payment Methods 56

    How to Survey Customers' Payment Preferences 59

    Examples of Successful Businesses Using Various Payment Options 61

Chapter 5 65

Offering Discounts 65

    Benefits of Offering Discounts 65

    Types of Discounts and Special Offers 67

    Timing and frequency of discounts 69

    Case Studies for Effective Discount Strategies 71

Chapter 6 77

Bundling Products 77

    Definition and Advantages of Product Bundling 77

    Example of Successful Product Bundles 79

    How to Make Appealing Bundles for Customers 81

    Case Studies for Successful Bundling Strategies 84

Chapter 7 88

Streamlined Products and Services 88

    Benefits of Streamlined Product Range......................89

    Differences in Large and Small Businesses 92

    Case Studies for Successful Streamlining 94

Chapter 8..100

Offering a Money Back Guarantee.............................100

    Importance of Building Customer Trust..................100

    Create a Money-Back Guarantee Policy 102

    Communication of guarantees to customers............104

    Examples of Effective Money Back Guarantees.....105

Chapter 9..111

Keeping an Eye on Trends..111

    The Value of Keeping Up with Market Trends and Purchase Behavior 112

    Case Studies of Companies That Respond to Trends 118

Chapter 10..124

Making Use of Technology 124

    The advantages of data analytics.............................132

    Important Domains in Sales Data Analytics............133

    Examples of Sales Strategies Enhanced by Technology 135

Chapter 11..139

Education and Training 139

The Value of Constant Sales Education 139
Focus Areas for Training Initiatives 141
Strategies for Selling 142
Instances of Successful Training Initiatives 146

Chapter 12 150
Establishing Robust Connections 150
The Value of Developing Relationships in Sales 150
Methods for Developing Stronger Customer Connections 151
Case Studies of Effective Relationship Development 154

Chapter 13 158
Establishing and Reaching Sales Objectives 158
Clear Sales Objectives Are Essential 159
Techniques for Creating Achievable and Realistic Goals 160
Typical Sales KPIs 162
Techniques for Encouraging and Monitoring Team Development 164
An overview of the main ideas 167

Introduction

In today's competitive corporate world, boosting sales while lowering expenses is critical to assuring long-term growth and profitability. Sales teams play an important role in driving revenue, making their tactics and actions critical to a company's success. This document delves into 13 effective tactics that can help sales teams increase sales, improve customer satisfaction, and eventually contribute to the overall growth of their organizations.

Importance of Sales and Cost Management in Business Growth
Sales and cost management are two essential components of corporate growth. Effective sales methods increase revenue by acquiring new consumers and encouraging repeat purchases from current clients. On the other hand, effective cost management ensures that increasing income translates into higher profitability by reducing wasteful expenses. Together, these aspects form a balanced approach to financial health and corporate growth.

Sales are a revenue driver.

Most firms rely on sales as their primary revenue stream. A company's financial stability is determined by its capacity to sell products or services on a continuous and successful basis. High sales statistics not only produce immediate cash, but also help to drive long-term growth by increasing market share and customer loyalty. Companies with great sales performance are better positioned to invest in new prospects, develop, and maintain their competitiveness.

Cost Management and Profitability

While boosting revenue is critical, controlling costs is also necessary to ensure profitability. Effective cost management entails finding and removing inefficiencies, obtaining better terms with suppliers, and streamlining operational processes. Companies that maintain costs under control can increase their profit margins and reinvest savings in growth efforts such as R&D, marketing, and talent acquisition.

The Role of Sales Teams in Driving Revenue

Revenue generation is mostly the responsibility of sales teams. Their efforts have a direct impact on the company's bottom line, hence their performance is an important indicator of business success. Salespeople are in charge of locating potential customers, analyzing their needs, proposing solutions, and closing transactions. Aside from these fundamental activities, they play an important role in developing and sustaining customer connections, which are required for repeat business and referrals.

Salespeople as brand ambassadors

Sales teams are frequently the initial point of contact between a firm and its clients. They serve as brand ambassadors for the organization, representing its values, culture, and products. Effective salespeople may make a positive impression, generate trust, and promote loyalty, all of which help to increase long-term income.

Strategic Sales Management.

Sales managers and executives play a critical role in guiding their staff. They create sales strategy, set objectives, track performance, and coach and assist their teams. By integrating sales efforts with broader business goals, sales managers guarantee that their teams effectively contribute to the company's growth ambitions.

Overview of 13 Strategies for Increasing Sales

Sales teams can use a variety of techniques to increase revenue and sustain growth. Here are 13 proven techniques to boost sales and improve business performance:

1. Understand your customers.
2. Use the Sales Funnel Model.
3. Interact With Customers Online
4. Provide a variety of payment options.
5. Offer discounts.
6. Bundle Products
7. Streamline Products and Services.
8. Provide a money-back guarantee.
9. Track trends.

10. Leverage Technology.
11. Train and develop your sales team.
12. Build Strong Relationships.
13. Set and achieve sales goals.

These strategies take a variety of techniques, including customer interaction, product offerings, technology integration, and team development. Implementing these approaches can help sales teams improve their effectiveness, generate more income, and contribute to their organizations' overall success.

Understand Your Customers

Customers are a business's most precious asset. Understanding their wants, difficulties, desires, and concerns is critical to creating products and services that match their expectations. This thorough understanding can lead to increased client pleasure, loyalty, and, eventually, sales.

Identifying Customer Needs.

To effectively market to customers, it is critical to understand their needs. This involves:

Conducting market research to gain insight into client preferences.

Analyzing customer input from surveys, reviews, and social media platforms.

Interviews and focus groups are used to directly engage with customers.

Creating Customer Personas

Creating thorough client personas helps to visualize the target demographic. These personas should comprise demographics, purchasing habits, pain issues, and preferences. Sales teams can utilize personas to adjust their tactics and messaging to appeal to different consumer segments.

Anticipating Customer Concerns.

Understanding frequent client problems and objections enables sales teams to handle them proactively. Salespeople may increase trust and facilitate purchasing decisions by providing clear information, displaying product value, and delivering reassurance.

Anticipating Customer Concerns.

Understanding frequent client problems and objections enables sales teams to handle them proactively. Salespeople may increase trust and facilitate purchasing decisions by providing clear information, displaying product value, and delivering reassurance.

Follow the Sales Funnel Model.

The sales funnel model is an effective tool for visualizing the customer journey from first interest to ultimate transaction. Understanding and optimizing each stage of the funnel can lead to higher conversion rates and sales growth.

Stages of Sales Funnel

Awareness: Potential customers become aware of the company's offers.

Interest: Customers express interest by requesting more information.

Decision: Customers choose to purchase a product or service.

Action: A final purchase is made.

Optimizing the Sales Funnel.

To increase the effectiveness of the sales funnel:

Increase Awareness: Use marketing efforts, social media, and content marketing to attract new customers.

Cultivate Interest: Offer thorough product information, demonstrations, and client testimonials.

Facilitate Decision-Making: To encourage purchasing decisions, consider offering incentives such as discounts or free trials.

Ensure Easy Action: Make the purchasing process as simple and quick as feasible.

Monitoring Funnel Performance.

Regularly assessing the performance of each stage of the sales funnel allows you to find bottlenecks and opportunities for development. Sales teams can use analytics like conversion rates, lead times, and customer feedback to fine-tune their plans and improve the overall effectiveness of the funnel.

Interact with customers online.

In today's digital world, communicating with clients online is critical. Many consumers prefer to conduct research and interact with businesses via digital media before making a purchase.

Creating an Online Presence

Developing a strong internet presence involves:

Creating a User-Friendly Website: Make sure the website is easy to access, informational, and mobile-friendly.

Maintaining Active Social Media Accounts: Use channels such as Facebook, Twitter, Instagram, and LinkedIn to interact with customers.

Online assistance: To assist clients, provide live chat, email assistance, and a detailed FAQ section.

Engaging with customers

Effective online engagement involves:

Responding Promptly: Respond to consumer requests and comments immediately and professionally.

Creating Valuable Content: Share articles, videos, and infographics that are valuable to your audience.

Encouraging User-Generated Content: Encourage users to share their experiences and feedback online.

Leveraging Online Reviews

Online reviews have a huge influence on purchasing decisions. Encourage satisfied consumers to submit good evaluations and respond to negative feedback constructively. Monitoring and reacting to reviews helps to establish a trustworthy and reputable internet presence.

Provide a variety of payment options.

Offering numerous payment alternatives can encourage more clients to purchase from your firm. Customers have diverse payment preferences when it comes to their transactions.

Identifying the preferred payment methods

To determine what payment methods to offer:

First conduct surveys to better understand client preferences.

Secondly, examine competitors' payment alternatives.

And then follow industry trends and innovations in payment technologies.

Payment Options

Consider offering:

Credit/Debit Cards: Credit/debit cards are widely utilized and convenient for most clients.

Digital Wallets: Digital wallets include PayPal, Apple Pay, and Google Wallet.

Installment Plans: Installment plans allow clients to pay in smaller, more affordable sums over time.

Direct Bank Transfers: Direct bank transfers are secure and simple for large transactions.

Implementing Flexible Payment Solutions

Work with payment service providers to effortlessly incorporate these choices into your shopping process. Ensure that the payment gateway is safe, user-friendly, and capable of processing a variety of transaction types.

Offer discounts

Discounts are an efficient approach to encourage purchases and increase sales. They can attract new customers, increase repeat business, and reduce inventory.

Types of Discounts

There are various discount schemes, including:

Two for the Price of One: Encourages buyers to purchase more things.

Buy One, Get One Free: Increases the number of purchases.

Seasonal Promotions: Match discounts to holidays or seasonal activities.

Loyalty discounts: Offer exclusive bargains to repeat consumers.

Bundle products

Product bundling is selling many products at a discounted price, increasing the value of the customer's purchase and enticing them to buy more.

Benefits of Product Bundling

Increased Sales: Bundling can raise the average transaction value.

Enhanced Customer Experience: Offers clients a complete solution, increasing satisfaction.

Example of Successful Product Bundles

Technology Bundles: Selling a flat-screen TV along with a discounted sound system.

Service Bundles: A software package including several complementing applications.

How to Make Appealing Bundles for Customers.

Identify Complementary things: Select things that are naturally compatible.

Offer Attractive Discounts: Ensure that the bundled pricing represents a significant savings as compared to purchasing products separately.

Promote Bundles Effectively: Emphasize the bundle's benefits in marketing materials.

Chapter One

Understanding Your Customers.

Identifying the customer's needs, challenges, desires, and fears

In the area of sales and marketing, understanding your clients is the basis around which successful initiatives are built. Identifying client wants, difficulties, desires, and anxieties allows firms to adjust their products, services, and messages to appeal to their intended audience. This alignment not only improves consumer pleasure, but it also increases sales and promotes loyalty.

Identifying Customer Needs.

Customer demands are the critical requirements or issues that your product or service seeks to solve. These requirements can be functional, like the need for a consistent internet connection, or emotional, like the desire for security or status. Understanding these needs necessitates a thorough examination of the customer's daily activities, pain points, and expectations.

Functional Needs

Functional demands are the fundamental requirements that any product or service must meet. For example, a consumer purchasing a washing machine requires it to effectively clean clothes. Identifying these needs includes:

Product Functionality: Ensuring that the product fulfills the intended purpose consistently.
Usability: Usability means making sure the product is simple to use and accessible.
Support Services: Provides customer support for any concerns or questions.

Emotional Needs

Emotional demands extend beyond functionality and address the customer's feelings and experiences. These may include:

Security: The desire to feel safe and secure.

Recognition: Recognition is the desire for rank, distinction, or acknowledgment.

Belonging: Belonging is the desire to feel a member of a community or group.

Identifying Customer Challenges.

Customer challenges are impediments or difficulties that keep customers from reaching their objectives or meeting their needs. Identifying these issues allows firms to design solutions that ease these pain points, making their products or services more appealing.

Common Challenges

Complexity: This refers to products or services that are difficult to use or understand.

Cost: Expensive costs make it harder for buyers to afford the product or service.

Time: Time constraints prevent you from properly researching, purchasing, or using a product or service.

Accessibility: Difficulty in obtaining the product or service owing to location or availability.

Identifying Customer Desire

Customer desires are the needs or wishes that influence purchasing decisions. These desires frequently extend beyond fundamental needs, touching on goals, dreams, and lifestyle preferences. Understanding these aspirations can assist organizations in developing products and marketing messages that resonate at a deeper level.

Common Desires

Innovation: This is the desire for innovative, cutting-edge items that have advanced features or capabilities.

Convenience: Convenience is the desire for items or services that save time and effort.

Quality: A desire for high-quality, long-lasting, and dependable products.

Personalization: Personalization is the desire for products or services that are personalized to each individual's preferences and demands.

Identifying Customer Fears.

Customers' fears are the anxieties or concerns that may prevent them from purchasing a product or service. Addressing these worries in your marketing and sales methods will help you gain trust and increase conversions.

Common Fears

Purchase Risk: Concerns about squandering money on a product that may not live up to expectations.

Complexity: Fear of being unable to use the thing successfully.

Change: Fear of switching from a familiar product or service to a new one.

Commitment: Reluctance to enter into long-term commitments or subscriptions.

Methods to Gather Customer Insights
Understanding clients necessitates obtaining data and insights using a variety of ways. These insights aid in understanding needs, challenges, desires, and anxieties, enabling firms to make sound decisions.

Surveys

Surveys are an effective way to collect quantitative data from a large audience. They can take place online, by email, or in person, and can cover a wide range of topics.

Designing Effective Surveys

Clear objectives: Define what you hope to learn from the survey.

Target Audience: Ensure that the survey reaches the appropriate client segment.

Question Types: Use a variety of question types, including multiple-choice, Likert scale, and open-ended.

Length: Survey length should be kept concise to encourage completion.

Types of Surveys

Customer Satisfaction Surveys: Determine overall satisfaction with your product or service.

Product input Surveys: Collect specific input about a new or existing product.

Market research surveys: This help you understand broad market trends and customer preferences.

Best Practices.
Pre-test: Conduct a pilot survey to detect potential difficulties.
Incentives: Offer incentives such as discounts or entrance into a prize draw to encourage participation.
Follow-Up: Analyze the results and contact responders if needed for clarification.

Feedback Forms

Feedback forms are a more direct means to collect consumer feedback, and they are frequently utilized at the time of sale or following a service encounter. They provide qualitative data that can help identify specific difficulties or opportunities for improvement.

Implementing Feedback Forms

Accessibility: Make feedback forms simple to use and complete.

Simplicity: Keep forms brief and focused on important questions.

Timing: Hand out forms at the proper times, such as after a purchase or service encounter.

Questions to Include:

Satisfaction Rating: A basic scale for determining overall satisfaction.

Product/Service Experience: Questions on specific features of the product or service.

Suggestions for improvement: Include open-ended questions to encourage additional feedback.

Utilizing Feedback.

Analyze Trends: Search for common themes or reoccurring concerns.

Act on Insights: Make modifications based on the input you received.

Communicate Changes: Inform customers about any improvements made in response to their comments.

Customer Interviews.

Customer interviews provide in-depth, qualitative insights that surveys and feedback forms may miss. Direct talks with clients are used to delve deeply into their experiences, needs, and difficulties.

Conducting effective interviews

Preparation: Create a roadmap with essential questions while remaining flexible.

Environment: Conduct interviews in a comfortable environment, either in person or digitally.

Active Listening: Active listening involves listening more than speaking and encouraging open-ended responses.

Follow-up: Ask probing questions to acquire a better understanding.

Interview Techniques

Structured Interviews: Structured interviews involve asking a set list of questions to maintain consistency.

Semi-structured interviews: Ask a few important questions while allowing the conversation to flow spontaneously.

Unstructured Interviews: Allow the consumer to lead the discussion with minimal guidance.

Benefits of Customer Interviews

Detailed Insights: Improve your understanding of customer experiences and perspectives.

Personal Connection: Strengthen customer ties through direct interaction.

Identifying Unmet Needs: Discover needs or obstacles that may not be obvious using other ways.

Case Studies for Successful Customer Understanding

Case Study 1: Technical Innovations

Background: Tech Innovations, a business that specializes in smart home gadgets, wanted to know why their latest product, a smart thermostat, sold less than projected.

Methodology: They collected information through a series of customer interviews and surveys.

Findings:

Needs: Customers desired a thermostat that was simple to install and use.

Challenges: Many people found the installation method overly complicated.

Desires: Integration with existing smart home systems was highly desired.

Fears: Potential consumers were anxious about the product's compatibility and level of support.

Actions Taken:

First, start with Step-by-step instructions and videos were used to simplify the installation process.

Secondly, Ensured interoperability with common smart home systems.

Thirdly, Enhanced customer support with specialist installation assistance.

Results: Sales climbed by 30% in six months, and customer satisfaction levels improved dramatically.

Case Study 2: Healthy Foods

Background: Healthy Eats, a meal delivery service, wants to improve client retention and identify the characteristics that influence repeat purchases.

Methodology: They used feedback questionnaires at several consumer touchpoints and held in-depth interviews with long-term customers.

Findings:

Needs: Customers requested convenient, healthful lunch options.

Challenges: Some consumers felt the meal selection was limited.

Desires: There was a desire for more customized food planning.

Fears: Questions regarding the freshness and quality of the ingredients.

Actions Taken:

First, the list of choices was expanded to cover a greater range of meals.

Secondly, meal plans are now customizable.

Thirdly, Improved packaging to keep ingredients fresher.

Results: Customer retention rates climbed by 20%, and average order values increased as customers chose tailored plans.

Case Study #3: Fashion Forward

Background: Fashion Forward, an online boutique, intended to improve customer experience and increase sales by better understanding their target group.

Methodology: They gathered insights using a combination of online surveys and social media participation.

Findings:

Needs: Customers want fashionable, cheap fashion options.

Challenge: Finding the appropriate size and fit online can be difficult.

Desires: Seeking special, limited-edition things.

Fears: Concerns regarding the return policy and the trouble associated with returns.

Actions Taken:

Added a detailed sizing guide and virtual try-on options.

Next, Launched limited-edition collections to increase exclusivity.

Lastly, the return process has been simplified with free returns and expanded return terms.

Results: Online sales climbed by 25%, while the return rate fell as buyers made better educated purchases.

Understanding your clients is a continual process that requires constant involvement and change. Businesses that identify client wants, difficulties, aspirations, and anxieties may create goods, services, and strategies that actually resonate with their target audience. Surveys, feedback forms, and customer interviews are all essential tools for driving business decisions and increasing customer satisfaction and loyalty.

The case examples presented in this chapter show the practical benefits of investing in customer understanding. Businesses that prioritize their customers' needs and preferences are more likely to succeed, whether by streamlining difficult processes, providing tailored options, or increasing customer service. As we progress through this book, we will look at other tactics that build on this core understanding to help sales teams grow revenue and establish long-term client connections.

Chapter 2

Using the Sales Funnel Model

Explanation of Sales Funnel Stages

The sales funnel model is an important tool for understanding and optimizing the customer journey, from initial awareness to final purchase. It illustrates the steps a potential consumer takes before completing a purchase, allowing firms to modify their marketing and sales efforts accordingly. The sales funnel is often separated into four phases: awareness, interest, decision, and action.

Awareness

The Awareness stage is the top of the funnel, where potential buyers first learn about your product or service. This stage focuses on gaining attention and bringing people to your brand. Customers may not have a specific need or interest in your product at this point; all they know is that it exists.

Key Objectives

Visibility: Improve brand recognition and reach a larger audience.

Education: Inform potential clients about your offerings and the industry.

Strategies for Optimization

Content Marketing: Create useful, educational content, like as blog articles, videos, and infographics, to attract and educate potential clients.
Social Media Engagement: Use social media channels to publish content, communicate with consumers, and create a community for your brand.
Search Engine Optimization (SEO): Improve your website and content's ranking in search engine results, allowing visitors to find you more easily.
Sponsored Advertising: Use sponsored ads on sites such as Google Ads, Facebook, and Instagram to reach a wider audience quickly.

Examples

Company increased brand awareness by releasing a series of instructional blog pieces that were extensively shared on social media, resulting in a 50% increase in website traffic. While Company B used targeted Facebook advertisements to reach new audiences, resulting in a large increase in brand recognition and leads.

Interest

During the Interest stage, potential clients express genuine interest in your product or service. They seek additional information, interact with your content, and begin to examine how your services can fulfill their needs.

Key Objectives

Engagement: Promote greater engagement with your audience.

Education: Provide in-depth information about your products or services.

Strategies for Optimization

Email Marketing: Collect leads via sign-up forms and nurture them with useful and personalized email campaigns.

Webinars and Live Demos: Use webinars or live product demonstrations to deliver detailed information and answer queries in real time.

E-books and whitepapers: Provide downloadable content with extensive insights and value, encouraging potential consumers to share contact information.

Retargeting advertisements: Retargeting advertisements remind visitors of your product or service after they leave your website, ensuring that your brand remains top-of-mind.

Examples

Company C witnessed a 40% boost in lead engagement by providing a free e-book outlining industry best practices and collecting crucial contact information. While company D increased interest in their software solution by holding weekly live demos, which led to improved engagement rates and more qualified prospects.

Key Objectives

Trust Building: Gain credibility and trust from potential consumers.

Persuasion: Convince prospects that your product or service is the best fit for their requirements.

Strategies for Optimization

Customer Testimonials and Reviews: To increase trust and credibility, showcase good customer feedback and success stories.

Case Studies: Provide extensive case studies showing how your product or service has successfully solved comparable challenges for previous consumers.

Free Trials and Samples: Provide free trials or samples so that potential clients can see the value of your product firsthand.

Comparisons and Competitor Analysis: Use explicit comparisons to highlight your advantages over competitors.

Examples

Company E raised conversion rates by 30% after including client testimonials and thorough case studies on their website. Company F saw a 25% increase in sales after offering a free 30-day trial, which allowed clients to sample the product's benefits before making a purchase.

The Action stage is at the bottom of the funnel, where potential customers make their final choice to buy. This step focuses on the actual transaction and delivering a seamless, good experience.

Action

The Action stage is at the bottom of the funnel, where potential customers make their final choice to buy. This step focuses on the actual transaction and delivering a seamless, good experience.

Key Objectives

Conversion: Turn leads into paying consumers.

Client Satisfaction: Create a smooth purchasing procedure to increase client satisfaction.

Strategies for Optimization

Simplified Checkout Process: Streamline the checkout process to reduce friction and cart abandonment rates.

Clear calls to action (CTAs): Use simple and appealing CTAs to direct customers through the purchasing process.

Multiple Payment Options: Provide a number of payment ways to accommodate diverse client preferences.

Post-Purchase Follow-Up: Contact clients after the purchase to confirm their contentment and encourage repeat business.

Examples

Company G reduced cart abandonment by 20% by streamlining the checkout process and providing several payment methods. Company H raised recurring orders by 15% by sending effective post-purchase follow-up emails that thanked customers and suggested new products.

Strategies for Optimizing Each Stage
Optimizing the Awareness Stage.

Content Marketing

Creating high-quality, useful content that speaks to your target audience's interests and pain areas is critical. Blog posts, articles, videos, and infographics can all help to drive traffic to your website and introduce new clients to your business.

Social Media Engagement

Active participation on social media sites can greatly increase brand visibility. Share information, engage in conversations, and use targeted adverts to reach a larger audience. Respond to comments and communications from followers in a timely manner.

SEO

Optimizing your website for search engines guarantees that your content is easily accessible. Use relevant keywords, build high-quality backlinks, and make sure your website's technical SEO is up to par. Regularly update your material to keep it current and relevant.

Paid advertising.

Investing in sponsored advertising can significantly increase your visibility. Platforms such as Google Ads, Facebook Ads, and Instagram Ads allow you to target certain demographics, ensuring that your ads reach the intended audience. Monitor ad performance and adapt strategy to maximise ROI.

Optimizing the Interest Stage.

Email Marketing

Email marketing is an efficient method for nurturing leads. Capture email addresses via sign-up forms and provide valuable information in exchange, such as newsletters, e-books, or exclusive discounts. Segment your email list to send targeted and relevant messages to various audience segments.

Webinars and Live Demos

Hosting webinars or live demos allows you to present potential clients with detailed information about your products or services. These meetings enable real-time contact while addressing individual queries and concerns, hence increasing confidence and trustworthiness.

E-books and whitepapers

Offering digital information, such as e-books and whitepapers, can help your business establish itself as an industry thought leader. Ensure that this content is thorough and adds actual value, enticing prospects to share their contact information in order to access it.

Retargeting Ads

Retargeting advertisements can keep your brand in the minds of potential clients who have previously visited your website. These adverts serve as a reminder of your product or service, encouraging people to return and go through the sales funnel.

Optimizing the Decision Stage

Customer testimonials and reviews.

Showcasing favorable customer testimonials and reviews can have a big impact on potential consumers' decision-making. Highlighting delighted customers' experiences can help to establish trust and provide social proof that your product is beneficial.

Case Studies

Detailed case studies demonstrating how your product or service has successfully handled challenges for previous clients might be persuasive. Include concrete metrics and outcomes to demonstrate the practical value of your offerings.

Free Trials and Samples.

Offering free trials or samples helps potential clients to try out your goods or service firsthand. This can lower perceived risk and encourage customers to make a purchase after seeing the value firsthand.

Comparisons and Competitive Analysis

Making precise comparisons between your product and competitors will assist potential buyers grasp your distinct value proposition. Highlight the major benefits and differentiators that make your product the better option.

Optimizing the action stage

Simplified Checkout Process

A simplified checkout procedure decreases friction and the possibility of cart abandonment. Keep the procedure simple, with as few stages as possible, and provide clear directions and help throughout.

Clear calls to action (CTAs)

Use clear and appealing CTAs to direct potential customers through the purchasing process. Make it simple for customers to take the next step, whether it's adding a product to their cart, finishing the transaction, or signing up for a service.

Multiple payment options

Offering a variety of payment alternatives caters to varied consumer preferences and boosts the likelihood of a successful sale. Include payment choices such as credit/debit cards, digital wallets, and installment plans to meet a variety of demands.

Post-purchase follow-up

Following up with clients after their purchase can increase satisfaction and encourage repeat business. Send thank-you letters, solicit feedback, and provide extra product recommendations or discounts for future transactions.

Example of Effective Sales Funnel Implementation
Example 1: E-commerce Retailer.

Company Overview: An online clothes shop striving to boost sales and enhance the consumer experience.

Awareness Stage

Strategy: Increased brand visibility through social media advertising and influencer partnerships.

Outcome: Increased website traffic by 40% and created a large number of new leads.

Interest Stage

Strategy: Launched a series of engaging blog pieces and fashion advice, accompanied by a targeted email marketing campaign.

Outcome: Improved contact with potential consumers, resulting in a 25% increase in email subscribers.

The decision stage

Strategy: Their website now includes customer testimonials, detailed size guides, and high-quality product photographs.

Outcome: Conversion rates increased by 30% as potential consumers gained confidence in their purchasing decisions.

Action Stage

Strategy: Simplified the checkout process and provided several payment choices, including buy-now, pay-later.

Outcome: Cart abandonment was reduced by 20%, while overall sales increased.

Example 2: SaaS Company.

Company Overview: A SaaS company that offers project management tools.

During the awareness stage, a content marketing strategy was implemented to promote project management best practices through blog posts and whitepapers.

Outcome: Their website's organic traffic increased by 50%.

Interest Stage

Strategy: Held weekly webinars to highlight the software's capabilities and benefits, followed by personalized email follow-ups.

Outcome: Increased lead engagement and produced more qualified leads for the following round.

Decision Stage

Decision Stage Strategy: Provided a 30-day free trial and showcased client success stories on their website.

Outcome: Trial sign-ups increased by 35%, and trial-to-paid membership conversion rates improved.

Action Stage

Strategy: Streamlined onboarding with step-by-step tutorials and 24/7 client assistance.

Outcome: Increased customer happiness and retention, leading to a better lifetime value.

Example 3: B2B manufacturing.

Company Overview: A B2B manufacturing company that specializes in industrial equipment.

Awareness Stage

Strategy: Attended industry trade fairs and invested in SEO to boost their internet visibility.

Outcome: They increased their reach and created a significant number of new leads.

Interest Stage

Strategy: Created thorough product brochures and technical instructions that were delivered via email marketing and direct mail.

Outcome: Potential consumers were engaged, and the quality of leads entering the decision-making stage improved.

The decision stage

Strategy: Offered on-site demonstrations and free consultations to address unique customer needs and concerns.

Outcome: Conversion rates increased as candidates had hands-on exposure with the equipment.

Action Stage

Strategy: Provided flexible financing and a streamlined purchasing process.

Outcome: Increased sales and shortened the sales cycle, making it easier for customers to complete their transactions.

The sales funnel model enables firms to understand and optimize each stage of the client experience. Companies can improve their marketing and sales efforts by customizing strategies to the specific demands and behaviors of potential customers at each stage (Awareness, Interest, Decision, and Action), resulting in improved conversion rates and revenue growth. The examples offered show how different firms can implement and profit from a well-optimized sales funnel, resulting in increased engagement, higher customer happiness, and long-term business success.

Chapter 3

Communicating with Customers Online

Importance of Online Presence.
In today's digital world, having an online presence is critical for organizations of all sizes and sectors. The internet has changed the way businesses communicate with their clients, with the majority of interactions now taking place online. This chapter will look at the importance of having an online presence, several venues for consumer connection, best practices for online communication, and case studies that show successful online engagement.

Enhancing Visibility and Reach

An internet presence enables firms to access a worldwide audience, considerably exceeding the geographical limits of conventional stores. With billions of internet users globally, businesses may use digital platforms to increase visibility, attract new consumers, and raise brand awareness. This reach is especially essential for small and medium-sized businesses (SMEs), which may lack the resources to run large traditional advertising campaigns.

Building Trust and Credibility

A strong internet presence contributes to the establishment of trust and credibility among potential clients. A well-designed website, active social media presence, and excellent online reviews help to project a professional image. Customers frequently conduct research online before making a purchase, and a great online presence can affect their decision-making process. Transparency, reactivity, and the supply of valuable content are critical components in developing confidence.

Facilitating Customer Engagement

Digital platforms provide several options to interact with clients. Businesses can utilize social media, websites, and live chat tools to communicate with customers in real time, offering prompt assistance and tailored service. This level of participation can greatly improve client happiness and loyalty, resulting in greater revenue and long-term connections.

Collecting customer insights

An internet presence also allows firms to learn crucial information about their clients. Analytics systems monitor user behavior, preferences, and feedback, enabling businesses to better customize their products, services, and marketing campaigns to match client needs. These insights are crucial for making informed business decisions and being competitive in the marketplace.

Platforms for Customer Interaction
Social Media

Social media platforms have transformed how businesses interact with customers. Platforms such as Facebook, Instagram, Twitter, LinkedIn, and TikTok provide numerous opportunities to engage, share content, and develop communities. Each platform has distinct features and user demographics, allowing firms to tailor their approach to their intended audience.

Facebook

Facebook is a versatile medium for reaching a large audience. Businesses may set Facebook pages, submit updates, share content, and run targeted advertisements. Facebook Groups also allow you to create groups around certain interests or items, which promotes deeper involvement.

Instagram

Instagram is perfect for visually oriented marketing. Businesses may upload photographs and videos, use Stories for real-time updates, and use IGTV to create longer-form video content. Instagram's purchasing features allow for direct sales on the site, making it an effective e-commerce tool.

Twitter

Twitter allows for real-time communication and participation. Businesses may easily post news, updates, and content, communicate with customers via answers and direct messages, and participate in popular conversations using hashtags. Twitter's brevity makes it ideal for sending brief, effective messages.

LinkedIn

LinkedIn is a professional networking platform that is great for B2B marketing and industry-specific content. Businesses can publish content, advertise job openings, and connect with industry leaders. LinkedIn Groups provide conversations and networking within specialized professional communities.

TikTok

TikTok is a rapidly developing platform recognized for its short, captivating videos. It's very popular among younger audiences. Businesses can generate unique, entertaining content to raise brand awareness and run tailored advertisements to attract specific groups.

Websites

A company website acts as the hub for an organization's internet presence. It offers detailed information about products, services, and the firm itself. A well-designed, user-friendly website has a tremendous impact on customer perceptions and conversion rates.

Essential Features

Home Page: The home page should provide a summary of the company and its offerings, with easy navigation to other pages.

Product/Service Pages: Individual pages for each product or service, including descriptions, pricing, and client feedback.

About Us: Learn about our company's history, mission, and team.

Contact Information: Contact information is easily accessible, including phone numbers, email addresses, and physical addresses.

Blog: A section for sharing relevant articles, updates, and industry insights.

E-commerce Functionality: For firms selling things online, an integrated e-commerce platform is required to facilitate transactions.

Live Chat

Customers can receive real-time assistance through live chat services on websites. This can dramatically improve the user experience by allowing customers to get fast answers to their questions without leaving the site or waiting for email responses.

Benefits of Live Chat:

Instant Support: Responding to consumer inquiries quickly increases satisfaction and reduces the probability of cart abandonment.

Personalized Assistance: Chat agents can provide unique advise and solutions based on the customer's requirements.

Data Collection: Live chat exchanges provide useful information about frequent consumer complaints and preferences.

Increased Conversions: By answering concerns in real time, live chat can help visitors become paying customers.

Best Practices in Online Communication
Successful internet communication necessitates a planned approach and adherence to best practices. Here are some important principles to consider:

Be responsive.

In today's digital age, timely replies are critical. Customers want speedy responses, whether via social media, email, or live chat. Delayed reactions might result in frustration and missed opportunities. Automated answers or chatbots can help manage consumer expectations and give initial support when human representatives are unavailable.

Personalize Interactions.

Personalization improves the client experience and gives interactions greater significance. Use client names, refer to previous encounters, and customize recommendations depending on their preferences and behavior. CRM systems, which track customer data and interactions, can help with personalization.

Maintain consistent branding.

Consistency in branding across all online channels helps to strengthen your business identification. Use the same logos, colors, and tone of voice across your messages. Consistent branding increases awareness and trust, making your firm more distinctive to customers.

Provide valuable content.

Content is an effective way to engage clients and develop authority in your field. Share useful articles, how-to tips, videos, and infographics that cater to your clients' needs and interests. Valuable content not only attracts potential clients, but also keeps them interested and returning for more.

Be transparent and authentic

Transparency and authenticity are essential for developing trust with your audience. Be open about your products, services, and business procedures. Address any negative remarks or issues openly and swiftly. Authentic interactions establish a positive reputation and increase client loyalty.

Monitor and analyze performance

Use analytics tools to regularly monitor the performance of your online interactions. Monitor KPIs including response times, client satisfaction, engagement rates, and conversion rates. Analyze this data to identify areas for improvement and then adapt your plans accordingly.

Case Studies for Successful Online Engagement
Case Study #1: Starbucks

Starbucks is a global coffeehouse brand renowned for its robust internet presence and consumer interaction techniques.

Social Media Engagement

Starbucks uses social media channels such as Facebook, Instagram, and Twitter to communicate with customers and market their products. The company posts visually engaging material, communicates with followers via comments and messages, and executes interactive marketing.

My Starbucks Idea

Starbucks created "My Starbucks Idea," a platform for users to offer new goods, services, and shop enhancements. This effort not only provides useful insights but also helps clients feel respected and heard.

Outcome

Starbucks' online interaction techniques have resulted in a very loyal consumer base, improved brand exposure, and a consistent stream of new ideas that have been applied in stores throughout the world.

Case Study #2: Zappos

Company Overview: Zappos is an online shoe and clothes shop noted for providing excellent customer service.

Website & Live Chat

The Zappos website is user-friendly, with thorough product descriptions, customer reviews, and simple navigation. The company gives consumers with instant service via a live chat option, assisting them in finding the proper products and answering any questions.

Social Media Presence.

Zappos actively engages with their customers via social media sites. The company reacts to comments and messages quickly and shares content that matches its lighthearted and quirky brand image.

Outcome

Zappos' dedication to customer service and online interaction has given the company a reputation for excellence, resulting in high customer satisfaction, repeat business, and favorable word-of-mouth marketing.

Case Study #3: Airbnb

Company Overview: Airbnb is an online marketplace for housing and vacation experiences that connects hosts and tourists.

User-generated content.

Airbnb encourages its users to share their trip experiences and property images on social media. This user-generated content acts as genuine testimonials, encouraging others to book stays on the platform.

Social Media campaigns

Airbnb uses creative social media advertising to highlight unique properties and destinations. The brand also interacts with its fans by replying to comments, offering travel suggestions, and boosting user tales.

Website Experience

Airbnb's website provides a flawless booking experience, complete with detailed property listings, host reviews, and personalized recommendations based on customer preferences.

Outcome

Airbnb's emphasis on user-generated content and interactive social media campaigns has dramatically increased brand visibility and engagement. The platform's user-friendly website and tailored approach have led to its expansion and success in the competitive travel sector.

Case Study #4: Warby Parker

Startup Overview: Warby Parker is an optical startup noted for its novel approach to selling glasses online.

Virtual Try-On Feature

Warby Parker's website has a virtual try-on tool that lets buyers to view how different frames look on their faces by utilizing their computer or smartphone cameras. This interactive application improves the online shopping experience and enables customers to make confident purchasing decisions.

Social Media Engagement

Warby Parker uses social media to post style ideas, customer images, and behind-the-scenes content. The brand regularly communicates with its fans by replying to comments and messages and hosting contests and giveaways.

Customer Support

Warby Parker provides excellent customer assistance via live chat, email, and phone. The company's agents are well-known for their helpfulness and readiness to go above and beyond to assist consumers.

Outcome

Warby Parker's innovative use of technology and strong social media presence have helped drive its quick development and success. The company's customer-centric approach has led to high levels of satisfaction and loyalty.

Interacting with clients online is critical for modern organizations. An effective online presence increases visibility, fosters trust, promotes interaction, and gives useful customer insights. Businesses can make real connections with clients by utilizing platforms such as social media, websites, and live chat. Following best practices for online communication ensures that interactions are responsive, individualized, and in accordance with the brand's identity. Starbucks, Zappos, Airbnb, and Warby Parker's case studies show how effective online engagement can lead to increased customer pleasure, loyalty, and revenue. As the digital landscape evolves, organizations must stay nimble and imaginative in their online communication strategies in order to remain competitive and fulfill their customers' ever-changing expectations.

Chapter 4

Provides a Variety of Payment Options

Understanding Customers' Payment Preferences
In today's industry, the availability of a variety of payment alternatives can have a big impact on a customer's purchasing choice. Understanding customers' payment preferences is critical for businesses looking to improve the shopping experience, reduce cart abandonment, and ultimately increase sales. This chapter will discuss the importance of providing multiple payment methods, the many types of payment options available, how to poll customers about their payment preferences, and examples of organizations that have successfully used multiple payment options.

Importance of Payment Options
Enhancing the Customer Experience

Offering multiple payment alternatives improves the consumer experience by adding ease and flexibility. Customers love the ability to pick how they want to pay, which can make the shopping experience more efficient and fun.

Reducing cart abandonment

A sizable proportion of online buyers abandon their carts due to a lack of preferred payment options. Offering a variety of payment methods allows businesses to lower cart abandonment rates and convert more visitors into paying customers.

Increasing Trust and Credibility.

Providing well-known and trustworthy payment methods can boost a customer's trust in a firm. When customers realize that their chosen payment options are accessible, they feel more comfortable and confident about making purchases.

Expanding market reach.

Payment method preferences differ across areas and populations. Businesses that provide a diverse selection of payment methods can reach a larger audience, including international clients with varying payment preferences.

Different Payment Methods
Credit and Debit Cards

Credit and debit cards are among of the most popular and generally accepted payment methods. They are handy for customers and provide security features like fraud protection and chargebacks.

Credit Cards

Customers can use credit cards to make purchases that will be paid back later. They frequently come with rewards systems that can encourage spending. Businesses gain from accepting credit cards since they are widely used and have the potential to boost sales.

Debit Cards

Debit cards draw straight from a customer's bank account, allowing for a more instantaneous form of payment. Customers prefer them because they wish to avoid accruing debt. Accepting debit cards may appeal to budget-conscious customers.

Digital wallets

PayPal, Apple Pay, Google Wallet, and Samsung Pay are getting more popular due to their simplicity and security. These wallets digitally store payment information, allowing clients to complete transactions quickly and securely.

PayPal

PayPal is one of the most well-known digital wallets, providing secure payments and buyer protection. It is especially popular for online transactions, as it offers a convenient alternative to entering credit card information for each purchase.

Apple Pay & Google Wallet

Customers can pay with Apple Pay and Google Wallet on their cellphones. These wallets use near-field communication (NFC) technology to make contactless payments that are rapid and safe. They also provide additional levels of protection, such as biometric authentication.

Installment Plans

Installment plans, often known as buy-now-pay-later (BNPL) options, allow customers to pay for their products in installments. This can make higher-priced things more accessible and ease the financial load on clients.

Popular BNPL Providers.

Afterpay: Afterpay lets clients pay in four interest-free installments.

Klarna: Klarna offers a variety of payment methods, including pay later and slice it (monthly installments).

Affirm: Offers straightforward finance with no hidden fees and a clear payback schedule.

Other Payment Methods

Bank Transfers

Customers can pay securely using direct bank transfers, which are particularly useful for larger transactions. This method is often used in B2B transactions and in areas where bank transfers are the favored payment method.

Cryptocurrency

Cryptocurrencies like Bitcoin, Ethereum, and others are gaining popularity as payment mechanisms. They have cheap transaction fees and are especially appealing to tech-savvy users and those interested in decentralization.

Cash on Delivery (CoD)

Cash on Delivery is a popular technique in some areas, particularly where faith in internet payment methods is low. It allows customers to pay in cash when they receive their items, guaranteeing that they only pay when the thing is in their possession.

How to Survey Customers' Payment Preferences

Understanding your clients' payment choices necessitates direct feedback. Surveys can provide significant insights into which payment options are most popular with your target audience.

Designing the Survey

Key Questions to Include:

Current Payment Methods: What payment methods do you currently utilize for both online and offline transactions?

Preferred Payment options: What are your preferred payment options for both online and offline shopping?

Payment Method Experience: How would you grade your overall experience with each payment method you use?

Barriers to Use: Are there any payment methods that you avoid using? If so, explain why.

Interest in New Payment Methods: Are there any payment methods that you would like us to offer?

Feedback on Existing Options: Do you have any feedback on the payment alternatives that we now offer?

Distribution Channels

Email Surveys: Send surveys to your customer email list.

Website Pop-ups: Use pop-up surveys on your website to solicit feedback from active users.

Social Media: Share survey links on social media to reach a larger audience.

In-store: For businesses with physical premises, provide printed surveys or digital kiosks where customers can provide feedback.

Analyzing the Survey Results

After you've gathered survey responses, analyze the data to uncover common preferences and patterns. Look for patterns in preferred payment methods, reasons to avoid, and curiosity in new possibilities. Use this data to make informed decisions about which payment options to implement or prioritize.

Examples of Successful Businesses Using Various Payment Options
Example 1: Amazon.

Company Overview: Amazon is a multinational e-commerce behemoth noted for its customer-centric strategy.

Payment Options Offered

Credit/Debit Cards: Accepts all major credit and debit cards.

Amazon Pay: Amazon Pay is a digital wallet that enables users to use payment methods saved in their Amazon accounts.

Installment Plans: Provides installment payment options for select items through relationships with BNPL suppliers.

Gift Cards: Accepts Amazon gift cards as payment.

Outcome

Amazon accommodates to varied customer preferences by providing a variety of payment alternatives, which improves convenience and reduces cart abandonment. The provision of payment plans makes higher-priced things more accessible, resulting in increased sales.

Example 2: Walmart.

Company Overview: Walmart is a worldwide retail firm that operates both physical stores and an extensive online presence.

Payment Options Offered

Credit/Debit Cards: Accepts all major credit and debit cards.

Walmart Pay: Walmart Pay is a mobile payment service built into the Walmart app.

PayPal: Allows customers to pay using their PayPal account.

Cash: Accepts cash for in-store purchases and Cash on Delivery for online transactions in some areas.

Installment Plans: Partners with BNPL providers such as Affirm to offer installment payment options.

Outcome

Walmart's numerous payment options appeal to a wide range of customers, providing ease and flexibility. The integration of Walmart Pay into the app simplifies the payment process, improving the overall shopping experience. The availability of payment plans stimulates the purchasing of more expensive things.

Example 3: Shopify.

Company Overview: Shopify is a popular e-commerce platform that helps businesses develop and manage online stores.

Payment Options Offered

Credit/Debit Card: Accepts all major credit and debit cards.

Shop Pay: Shop Pay is a simple and secure payment option built into Shopify stores.

Digital Wallets: Accepts digital wallets such as Apple Pay and Google Wallet.

Installment Plans: Shop Pay Installments provide interest-free payments over time.

Alternative Payments: Accepts other methods such as cryptocurrency and bank transfers.

Outcome

Shopify offers flexibility to both merchants and customers by accepting a variety of payment methods. Shop Pay Installments have been particularly effective at increasing average order value and making larger purchases more manageable for clients.

Example 4: Peloton.

Company Overview: Peloton is a fitness company that offers high-end training equipment and subscription-based fitness sessions.

Payment Options Offered

Credit/Debit Cards: Accepts all major credit and debit cards.

Affirm: Collaborates with Affirm to provide installment payment plans.

Digital wallets: Accepts Apple Pay for quick and safe transactions.

Gift Cards: Accepts Peloton gift cards for both equipment and subscriptions.

Outcome

Peloton's installment payment alternatives through Affirm make their high-end fitness equipment more affordable to a wider range of customers. The integration of digital wallets improves the convenience of online purchases, resulting in higher customer satisfaction and sales.

In today's competitive economy, providing a number of payment alternatives is critical to satisfying customer expectations and boosting sales. Understanding client payment preferences and implementing a variety of payment methods allows businesses to improve the shopping experience, reduce cart abandonment, and develop trust and credibility. Customers' payment preferences might be surveyed to provide significant insights to help influence decision-making.

Amazon, Walmart, Shopify, and Peloton all exemplify how varied payment choices can be successfully implemented and have a beneficial influence on consumer satisfaction and sales. As technology evolves, businesses must remain adaptable and proactive in providing payment alternatives that best match their customers' expectations.

Chapter 5

Offering Discounts

Benefits of Offering Discounts

Offering discounts is a tried-and-true approach for attracting customers, increasing sales, and cultivating brand loyalty. Discounts can help firms get rid of old inventory, promote new products, and encourage repeat purchases. Here are some major advantages of offering discounts:

Increased sales volume.

Discounts can greatly increase sales by making things more cheap and appealing to a broader market. When clients believe they are getting a good deal, they are more likely to buy, which can lead to greater sales volume.

Customer Acquisition and Retention

Discounts are an efficient approach to attract new clients while keeping existing ones. New customers may be enticed to try a product or service due of a discount, whilst existing customers may enjoy the increased value and grow loyal to the brand.

Enhanced Brand Awareness

Offering discounts can create excitement and boost company visibility. Promotions can be shared on social media, included in marketing efforts, and disseminated through word-of-mouth, all of which assist to raise brand recognition and offerings.

Inventory Management

Discounts can help businesses manage their inventory more effectively by encouraging the sale of slow-moving or surplus items. This can free up storage space and lower holding costs, making it easier to launch new items.

Competitive advantage

Discounts can provide a major competitive advantage. By providing better offers, firms can attract price-sensitive clients who would otherwise prefer a competitor's goods.

Increased average order value

Customers might be encouraged to spend more by offering strategically tailored discounts, such as buy-one-get-one-free or free gifts with purchase. This can raise the average order value and enhance overall income.

Types of Discounts and Special Offers
Businesses can provide a variety of discounts and special deals to attract certain customer segments and achieve specific marketing objectives. Here are a few popular types:

Get two for the price of one

This form of deal, commonly known as "buy one, get one free" (BOGO), encourages customers to make larger purchases by providing an additional product at no additional cost. It is especially useful for things that customers may buy in bulk, such as food, household goods, or personal care products.

Buy one, get one free

Similar to the two-for-one promotion, this bargain entices buyers by including a free product with their purchase. It can assist boost sales volume and is especially enticing when used on consumable goods or those with a short shelf life.

Free gifts with purchase.

Offering a complimentary gift with a purchase can increase the perceived value of a customer's order, encouraging them to buy. The present could be a tiny, complimentary item or a trial of a new product. This method can also assist introduce clients to new products that they may not have considered before.

Percentage Discounts

Customers can easily grasp percentage discounts, such as 10%, 20%, or 50% off. They can be used on specific items, categories, or entire orders, making them an adaptable promotional tool.

Dollar Amount Discounts

Dollar amount discounts, such as $5 off a $50 purchase, provide a clear incentive for customers to spend a specific amount in order to obtain the discount. This form of discount can boost spending and raise the average order value.

Seasonal and Holiday Discounts

Seasonal and holiday discounts take advantage of peak shopping seasons. Back-to-school discounts, Black Friday specials, and Christmas advertising are some examples. These discounts can result in considerable sales during busy shopping seasons.

Loyalty discounts

Loyalty discounts reward repeat consumers for their continuous patronage. This can include unique discounts for loyalty program members, birthday discounts, or special incentives for customers who have purchased a specific number of times.

Flash sales

Flash sales are short-term promotions that generate a sense of urgency and stimulate fast purchasing. These promotions can be promoted by email, social media, or the company's website and frequently provide big discounts for a limited time.

Bundle Discounts

Bundle discounts provide a lower price when customers purchase many items together. This can inspire customers to purchase additional products, and it is especially beneficial for things that are frequently used together, such as electronics and accessories.

Timing and frequency of discounts

The time and frequency with which discounts are applied can have a significant impact on their effectiveness. Here are some factors for whether and how frequently to give discounts.

Key Shopping Seasons

Offering discounts during peak shopping seasons, such as the holiday season, back-to-school sales, or end-of-year clearance sales, can have a significant influence. Customers are more likely to shop at these periods, and they are looking for great discounts.

Product Lifecycle

When considering discounts, consider the product's lifespan. For example, offering discounts on older models when newer versions are available can aid in inventory clearance. Seasonal products can also receive discounts at the end of their peak season.

Consumer Behavior

Understanding client behavior and buying habits might help you determine the optimum times to provide discounts. For example, if customers are more likely to shop in the start of the month after payday, offering discounts during this time can be more beneficial.

Competitor Activity

Keep a watch on how and when competitors offer discounts. Offering discounts when competitors do not can give your company a competitive advantage. In contrast, matching or exceeding competitors' discounts during major sales events might help keep market share.

Frequency of discounts

While frequent discounts might increase sales, delivering them too frequently can devalue your products and teach customers to wait for discounts before making a purchase. Strike a balance by providing regular but not continual discounts, and consider employing loyalty programs to encourage repeat consumers without constantly lowering costs.

Case Studies for Effective Discount Strategies
Case Study #1: Macy's

Company Overview: Macy's is a well-known American department store company that sells a wide range of products such as apparel, accessories, home goods, and makeup.

Discount Strategy

Macy's routinely offers percentage discounts, seasonal promotions, and loyalty program discounts to entice shoppers. The corporation also uses seasonal sales events like Black Friday and Cyber Monday to provide deep discounts and promote large sales volumes.

Implementation

Seasonal Sales: Macy's offers huge sales events during peak shopping seasons, providing significant discounts on a wide range of merchandise.

Loyalty Program: Macy's Star benefits program provides unique discounts and benefits to habitual shoppers, encouraging repeat purchases.

Seasonal Promotions: The corporation executes massive advertising efforts to promote seasonal sales events, building anticipation and increasing visitors to its stores and website.

Outcome

Macy's smart use of discounts has assisted the corporation in attracting and retaining customers, increasing sales during peak shopping seasons, and establishing a loyal client base via its rewards program.

Case Study #2: Amazon Prime Day

Amazon is the world's largest online retailer, providing a wide range of items and services.

Discount Strategy

Amazon Prime Day is an annual sales event reserved exclusively for Amazon Prime subscribers. The event offers limited-time discounts on thousands of products from various categories.

Implementation

Prime Membership: The event is only available to Prime subscribers, which encourages more users to sign up for the subscription program.

Limited-Time discounts: Amazon offers lightning discounts and special promotions that last only a short time, generating a sense of urgency and promoting speedy purchases.

Wide Range of Discounts: Wide Range of Discounts: Discounts are available on a wide range of products, attracting a diverse audience and increasing overall sales volume.

Outcome

Amazon Prime Day has grown to become one of the year's most successful shopping occasions, earning billions of dollars in sales. The event enhances Amazon Prime membership sign-ups, increases consumer loyalty, and drives large sales.

Case Study #3: Starbucks

Company Overview: Starbucks is a global coffeehouse chain recognized for its high-quality coffee and customer-centric strategy.

Discount Strategy

Starbucks attracts and retains customers by offering loyalty program discounts, seasonal promotions, and limited-time specials.

Implementation

Starbucks Rewards: The loyalty program provides users with discounts, free drinks, and other benefits based on their purchasing history.

Seasonal Promotions: Starbucks provides seasonal specials, including discounts on holiday-themed drinks and products.

Limited-Time Offers: The company routinely launches limited-time promotions, such as buy-one-get-one-free bargains on beverages.

Outcome

Starbucks' discount strategy has proven to establish a loyal customer base, encourage repeat visits, and boost sales during peak periods. The loyalty program, in particular, has been extremely effective in increasing customer loyalty and driving repeat purchases.

Case Study #4: Sephora

Company Overview: Sephora is an international retailer of beauty and personal care items noted for its diverse selection of premium brands.

Discount Strategy

Sephora attracts and retains customers by offering loyalty program discounts, seasonal deals, and promotional events.

Implementation

Beauty Insider Program: Sephora's loyalty program provides members with unique discounts, early access to sales, and birthday presents.

Seasonal Sales: The corporation runs large sales events throughout peak shopping seasons, such as the annual VIB sale, where loyalty club members receive significant discounts.

Promotional Events: Sephora hosts a variety of promotional events, such as gift-with-purchase offers and brand-specific discounts, to increase sales and introduce customers to new products.

Outcome

Sephora's discount strategy has helped it create a strong and loyal client base, improve sales during peak seasons, and introduce customers to new products. The Beauty Insider program, in particular, has been extremely effective at increasing consumer loyalty and encouraging repeat purchases.

In conclusion, offering discounts is an effective approach for growing sales, attracting new consumers, and retaining existing ones. Offering discounts improves the consumer experience, reduces cart abandonment, builds confidence and credibility, and improves inventory management. Understanding the various sorts of discounts and special deals allows firms to adjust their strategies to specific marketing goals and customer preferences.

Discount schemes require precise timing and frequency to be effective. Offering discounts during peak shopping seasons, aligning with product lifecycles, knowing customer behavior, and tracking rival activity can all help them have a bigger impact. Businesses should be wary about offering discounts too regularly, as this might devalue products and reduce profit margins.

The case studies of Macy's, Amazon Prime Day, Starbucks, and Sephora demonstrate the power of well-planned discounting methods. These businesses have effectively leveraged discounts to attract and keep customers, increase sales during busy seasons, and foster strong customer loyalty through loyalty programs and unique deals.

In conclusion, providing discounts is an important element in a company's marketing arsenal. When handled wisely, discounts can result in significant revenue growth, increased brand recognition, and long-term consumer loyalty. Understanding consumer wants and preferences allows firms to develop discount strategies that benefit both the client and the company, assuring long-term success in a competitive environment

Chapter 6

Bundling Products

Definition and Advantages of Product Bundling

What is product bundling?

Product bundling is a marketing approach in which various items or services are combined and sold as a single unit at a reduced price. This strategy is meant to deliver more value to clients while persuading them to buy more things than they originally planned.

Benefits of Product Bundling

Increased sales and revenue.

Bundling products can increase sales volumes by enticing buyers to purchase many items in one transaction. This increase in average order value has the potential to dramatically improve a company's total revenue.

Improved customer perception of value

Customers view bundles to provide more value for their money. Customers believe they are making a wise investment when they acquire many things at a discounted price, which can increase their overall happiness.

Inventory Management

Product bundling improves inventory management efficiency. Businesses can reduce excess inventory and increase inventory turnover by pairing slower-moving items with popular ones.

Competitive advantage

Offering innovative and appealing bundles can set a company apart from its competitors. It gives buyers a compelling reason to choose one brand over another, especially if the bundle addresses their needs more fully.

Simplified Decision-Making

Bundles can make the purchasing process easier for customers. Instead of selecting and purchasing individual products, buyers can pick for a bundle that fits several demands, making the shopping experience more convenient and time-saving.

Enhanced Cross-Selling Opportunities

Bundling enables firms to introduce clients to things that they might not have considered purchasing alone. This may result in increased awareness and future sales of these extra products.

Example of Successful Product Bundles
Technology Bundles

Television and Sound System

A television and a sound system make an excellent technological bundle. Electronics retailers sometimes package high-definition TVs with surround sound systems or soundbars to improve the viewing experience. This not only increases the perceived value of the purchase, but also guarantees that customers have everything they need for the best entertainment experience.

Example: Best Buy

Best Buy usually provides bundles that contain a TV, a soundbar, and occasionally extra peripherals such as HDMI cables or streaming devices. These bundles are billed as comprehensive home entertainment solutions, making them particularly appealing to clients wishing to enhance their installations.

Laptop with Software Package

Another effective technology bundle combines a laptop with important software programs. This could include an operating system upgrade, productivity applications like Microsoft Office, antivirus software, and extra accessories like a mouse or laptop bag.

For example, Apple

Apple frequently packages its MacBooks with software like Final Cut Pro and Logic Pro at a discount. These bundles are especially interesting to students and professionals who require powerful tools for creative projects.

Service bundles

Software Packages

Service bundles, particularly in the software business, are quite effective. These bundles frequently comprise a variety of software items that compliment one another, giving users with a complete solution.

Adobe Creative Cloud, as an example

Adobe Creative Cloud is a subscription service that includes over 20 software tools, including Photoshop, Illustrator, and Premiere Pro. This bundle gives creatives all the tools they need for design, video editing, and digital art at a lower cost than buying each product separately.

Telecommunication Services

Telecommunications firms frequently combine services like internet, television, and phone plans. These bundles are touted as providing convenience and savings because clients receive many critical services from a single source at a lower rate.

For example, Comcast Xfinity

Comcast Xfinity offers packages that include high-speed internet, cable TV, and home phone service. These packages cater to consumers' various needs while saving them a significant amount of money over purchasing each service separately.

How to Make Appealing Bundles for Customers.

To create enticing product bundles, you must first understand your customers' demands, then select the correct products to package, and finally market them successfully. Here are some ideas to help businesses create attractive bundles:

Understanding Customers' Needs

Conduct Market Research

Businesses should perform extensive market research before developing customer-friendly bundles. This can include conducting surveys, focus groups, and analyzing customer purchase data to determine which goods are frequently purchased together and what customers value the most.

Segment your audience

Different client segments may have varying wants and preferences. Businesses can adapt bundles to each segment's individual needs by segmenting the audience based on demographics, purchasing behavior, and preferences.

Choosing the Right Products

Complementary Products

The most effective bundles frequently include complimentary things that naturally go together. For example, a smartphone that comes with a protective case and a screen protector is a full solution for a new phone owner.

High and Low Demand Products

Combining high-demand products with low-demand commodities can help sell inventory that might otherwise go unsold. This strategy can be very useful for getting rid of obsolete merchandise while still offering value to the client.

Pricing Strategy

Offer genuine savings

Customers must believe that they are receiving a fair value when purchasing a package. Make sure that the combined price of the bundled products is less than the total cost of purchasing each item separately. To highlight the value offer, communicate the savings clearly to customers.

Tiered Bundles

Consider offering tiered bundles with varying pricing points. This can meet a variety of consumer budgets and needs. For example, a basic bundle may only have the essentials, whereas a premium bundle may include additional accessories or services.

Effective marketing

Highlight the benefits

Customers should be clearly informed of the bundle's benefits. This involves emphasizing the cost savings, convenience, and increased value clients get from purchasing the bundle rather than individual items.

Use visuals

Use appealing pictures in marketing materials to highlight the bundled products. High-quality photos and videos can help clients see how the products work together and increase the bundle's perceived value.

Limited Time Offers

Creating a sense of urgency can help boost purchases. Offer packages as limited-time deals to entice buyers to act fast. Highlighting the offer's limited availability might raise perceived value and urgency.

Case Studies for Successful Bundling Strategies

Case Study #1: Microsoft Office 365

Company Overview: Microsoft is a significant technology business that produces software, hardware, and services.

Bundling Strategy

Microsoft provides Office 365 as a subscription service that includes critical productivity tools such as Word, Excel, PowerPoint, and OneDrive cloud storage. The package is available for both personal and business use, with several pricing tiers to meet various requirements.

Implementation

Subscription Model: Office 365 is available on a subscription basis, ensuring continuous access to the most recent software upgrades and features.

Different tiers: The service is accessible in three tiers: Office 365 Personal, Office 365 Home, and Office 365 Business, each tailored to distinct user needs.

Online Integration: The bundle includes OneDrive online storage, which allows for seamless collaboration and access to data across several devices.

Outcome

The Office 365 bundle has been a huge success, offering customers with vital productivity tools at an affordable price. The subscription model generates recurrent revenue for Microsoft, while the various tiers and cloud integration appeal to a wide range of users.

Case Study #2: Nintendo Switch

Corporation Overview: Nintendo is a global consumer electronics and video game corporation best recognized for its innovative gaming systems and successful game titles.

Bundling Strategy

Nintendo frequently provides packages that include the Nintendo Switch console, popular game titles, and accessories. These bundles are intended to give a comprehensive gaming experience and increase the value proposition for customers.

Implementation

Game Bundles: Bundles frequently feature the Nintendo Switch console and a top-selling game, such as "Mario Kart 8 Deluxe" or "The Legend of Zelda: Breath of the Wild."

Accessory Bundles: Some bundles contain additional controllers, carrying cases, and screen protectors.

Limited Editions: Nintendo creates limited edition bundles based on popular game releases, which appeal to collectors and fans.

Outcome

Nintendo's bundling strategy has boosted console sales and increased attachment rates for game titles and accessories. The limited edition bundles provide additional excitement and urgency, resulting in great sales success.

Case Study #3: Meal Kit Delivery Services

Company Overview: Companies such as Blue Apron and HelloFresh provide meal kit delivery services, giving clients pre-portioned materials and recipes to prepare at home.

Bundling Strategy

Meal kit delivery providers bundle all of the components for many meals into a single box. These bundles provide convenience and variety, allowing clients to plan and prepare meals at home.

Case Study #4: Verizon

Verizon is a significant telecommunications corporation that offers internet, television, and telephone services.

Bundling Strategy

Verizon provides bundled bundles that include internet, TV, and phone services in one subscription. These bundles are intended to give full home connectivity options at a reduced cost compared to purchasing each service individually.

Implementation

Triple Play Bundles: These packages often contain high-speed internet, a variety of TV channels, and home phone service.

Promotional Pricing: Verizon provides promotional rates for the first year of service, making the bundles particularly appealing to new consumers.

Add-On Options: Customers can personalize their bundles with premium TV channels, faster internet speeds, and home security services.

Outcome

Verizon's bundling strategy has proven effective in attracting and maintaining consumers by providing complete and configurable home connectivity solutions. The promotional price and add-on choices offer flexibility and value, resulting in great customer satisfaction.

Product bundling is a potent approach for increasing sales, improving customer satisfaction, and gaining a competitive advantage in the market. Businesses can build compelling deals that improve customers' perceived value and convenience by analyzing their needs, selecting complimentary items, and marketing bundles successfully.

Companies such as Best Buy, Apple, Adobe, Comcast Xfinity, Microsoft, Nintendo, Blue Apron, and Verizon have used successful bundling methods, demonstrating the versatility and effectiveness of this technique across industries. These organizations have effectively used bundling to boost sales, manage inventories, and foster strong customer loyalty.

To summarize, product bundling is an important marketing technique for any organization. When applied properly, it can provide enormous benefits to both the organization and its customers, assuring long-term success and growth in a competitive market.

Chapter 7

Streamlined Products and Services

In a competitive market, firms frequently confront the issue of managing a wide range of products and services. While a diverse product offering can attract a large consumer base, it can also result in inefficiencies, increased expenses, and diluted brand identity. Streamlining products and services entails decreasing complexity by focusing on core offers that better fulfill client needs. This chapter investigates the benefits of streamlining, tactics for simplifying product offerings, and the differences in approach between large and small organizations, using case studies from successful streamlining programs.

Benefits of Streamlined Product Range
Enhanced operational efficiency

Reducing the quantity of products or services can greatly boost operational efficiency. Simplified options contribute to easier inventory management, manufacturing processes, and supply chain logistics. This efficiency can lead to cost savings, less waste, and faster responses to market changes.

Improved focus on core competencies

Streamlining enables firms to focus on their core skills. Companies that focus on their strengths can better manage resources, improve product quality, and provide superior customer service. This specialization can lead to a better market position and a greater competitive advantage.

Better inventory management

Inventory management is made easier by having a streamlined product line. It decreases the demand for large storage facilities and lowers the danger of overstocking or stockouts. This can result in better cash flow management and cheaper holding costs, hence increasing the bottom line.

Enhanced Customer Experience

Customers frequently value a simple buying experience. A streamlined product line can help clients find what they need, decreasing decision fatigue and enhancing satisfaction. Clear, focused product offerings can help to develop brand identity and loyalty.

Cost Savings

Simplifying product offerings can result in significant cost reductions. Reduced complexity in manufacturing, distribution, and marketing can result in lower operational costs. These cost savings can be reinvested in other areas of the organization, such as innovation, customer service, or marketing campaigns.

Faster time-to-market

Businesses may bring new items to market faster since they have fewer products to develop and launch. This adaptability can be critical in adapting to changing customer preferences and staying ahead of the competition.

Strategies to Simplify Product Offerings

Analyze sales data

A detailed review of sales data can reveal which goods perform well and which underperform. By focusing on high-margin, high-demand items, organizations can eliminate low-performing products that do not generate considerable revenue.

Understand the needs of the customers

Gathering and analyzing customer feedback on a regular basis can assist firms in determining which items or services their customers value the most. Surveys, focus groups, and customer evaluations can reveal customer preferences and problem issues, influencing judgments on which items to keep or cancel.

Implement a Pareto analysis

The Pareto Principle, sometimes known as the 80/20 rule, states that 80% of a company's revenues are typically generated by 20% of its goods. Businesses can streamline their products while maintaining income by identifying and focusing on this key 20%.

Focus on core products

Businesses should concentrate on core products or services that are consistent with their brand identity and strategic objectives. Companies that emphasize these main offerings can assure consistency and coherence in their market positioning.

Consolidate similar products

Combining similar items can decrease redundancy and simplify the product line. This entails integrating goods that provide similar functions or target the same client categories, while ensuring that each offering has a clear, differentiated value proposition.

Regularly review the product portfolio

A regular evaluation of the product portfolio is vital for keeping the offering simplified. This assessment should evaluate each product's performance, relevance, and profitability, ensuring that the portfolio evolves in accordance with market trends and corporate goals.

Differences in Large and Small Businesses

Large businesses

Complexity and Resources

Large companies typically have more sophisticated operations and a wider product line. They also have more resources to handle this complexity, such as sophisticated inventory management systems and large supply networks. However, due to the size of their operations, streamlining can be a more difficult and time-consuming task.

Market Reach

Large firms often cater to a broader and more diverse consumer base. Streamlining efforts must take into account the unique needs of different market segments, combining the desire for simplicity with the necessity to respond to a wide range of tastes.

Bureaucratic hurdles

Decision-making procedures in large businesses can be delayed due to bureaucratic barriers. Streamlining projects may necessitate substantial stakeholder alignment and consent, thereby delaying implementation.

Small businesses.

Agility and Flexibility

Small organizations are often more agile and adaptable, allowing them to execute streamlining measures faster. Their reduced size frequently results in fewer products and less complex activities, making the process easier.

Limited Resources

Small firms benefit from agility, yet they frequently have limited resources. Streamlining allows them to concentrate their efforts and resources on their most profitable items or services, maximizing their limited capacity.

Niche Focus

Small firms frequently target specific markets with specialized products or services. Streamlining operations can help them better cater to these unique markets, strengthening their niche positioning and client loyalty.

Case Studies for Successful Streamlining

Case Study #1: Apple Inc

Background

Apple Inc. is well-known for its streamlined product line. Despite being one of the world's top technological businesses, Apple has a very small product selection, focused on quality and innovation.

Streamlining Strategy

Focus on Core Products: Apple focuses on a few core product categories, including the iPhone, iPad, Mac, and Apple Watch. Each product line is meticulously chosen, with a finite number of models.

Simplicity in Design and Features: Apple products are well-known for their simplicity and usability. This emphasis on simplicity extends to their product line, ensuring that each item is unique and straightforward for clients to grasp.

Regular Product Reviews: Apple conducts regular product reviews and discontinues models that are obsolete or less popular. This guarantees that their product offerings remain current and in line with customer needs.

Outcome

Apple's simplified product portfolio has helped to strengthen its brand identification and consumer loyalty. Apple's concentration on core goods and simplicity has allowed it to sustain significant profit margins and market leadership in the technology industry.

Case Study #2: Starbucks

Background

Starbucks, a global coffeehouse business, experienced issues with a complex menu that was difficult for customers to browse, resulting in operational inefficiencies.

Streamlining Strategy

Starbucks launched a menu simplification campaign, lowering the number of options on its menu to focus on the core offers that were most popular with customers.

Operational Efficiency: The reduced menu enabled faster preparation times and increased store efficiency, resulting in shorter wait times and a better customer experience.

Focus on Customization: By reducing the menu, Starbucks was able to emphasize customization, allowing consumers to customize their drinks with a variety of alternatives and add-ons.

Outcome

The menu simplification program increased customer happiness and operational efficiency. Starbucks was able to strengthen its brand identity by focusing on core items and personalization, resulting in greater sales and consumer loyalty.

Case Study #3: McDonald's

Background

McDonald's, the world's largest fast-food company, saw dwindling sales and customer unhappiness as a result of an overly confusing menu.

Streamlining Strategy

Menu Rationalization: McDonald's developed a menu rationalization approach, which involved deleting less popular items and focusing on core offers such as the Big Mac, Quarter Pounder, and Chicken McNuggets.

Operational Improvements: Simplifying the menu reduced kitchen complexity, improved order accuracy, and sped up serving times.

Enhanced Marketing Focus: The reduced menu allowed McDonald's to focus its marketing efforts on its key goods, thereby reinforcing its brand image.

Outcome

Following the menu reduction, McDonald's sales and customer satisfaction improved. The company's focus on core products and operational efficiency helped it reclaim market share and increase profitability.

Case Study #4: General Motors (GM)

Background

General Motors, a leading automaker, experienced financial difficulties and a decline in market share as a result of its large and unfocused product line.

Streamlining Strategy

Brand Consolidation: General Motors simplified its brand portfolio by eliminating or selling less lucrative brands such as Pontiac, Saturn and Hummer. The corporation concentrated on its core brands, Chevrolet, GMC, Buick, and Cadillac.

Product Line Simplification: Within its main brands, GM decreased the number of models while focusing on high-demand areas including SUVs, trucks, and electric vehicles.

Operational Efficiency: By streamlining the product line, General Motors was able to streamline its manufacturing processes, decrease costs, and improve supply chain management.

Outcome

GM's restructuring efforts resulted in improved financial performance and a stronger market position. Focusing on key brands and high-demand areas allowed the company to better align its product offerings with customer preferences and market trends.

Conclusion

Streamlining products and services is a strategic approach that can lead to significant benefits for businesses of all sizes. By focusing on core offerings, simplifying operations, and enhancing customer experience, companies can achieve greater efficiency, cost savings, and market competitiveness.

The case studies of Apple, Starbucks, McDonald's, and General Motors illustrate the diverse ways in which businesses have successfully implemented streamlining initiatives. Whether through menu simplification, brand consolidation, or focusing on high-demand products, these companies have demonstrated the value of a streamlined approach in driving growth and profitability.

Ultimately, streamlining is about making strategic choices that align with the company's goals and customer needs. By regularly reviewing and optimizing their product and service offerings, businesses can stay relevant, efficient, and competitive in a dynamic market environment.

Chapter 8

Offering a Money Back Guarantee

In today's competitive environment, developing and keeping consumer trust is critical to corporate success. Offering a money-back guarantee is a great approach that businesses may use to boost customer confidence in their products and services. This chapter delves into the necessity of establishing customer trust, the process of developing an effective money-back guarantee policy, best practices for conveying guarantees to customers, and case studies of organizations that have successfully adopted money-back guarantees.

Importance of Building Customer Trust
Enhancing Customer Confidence

A money-back guarantee ensures that clients are making a risk-free transaction. This assurance can considerably boost client confidence, encouraging people to test new items or services without worrying about losing money if they are dissatisfied. Businesses that reduce perceived risk can enhance conversion rates and establish favorable customer relationships.

Differentiation from competitors

Offering a money-back guarantee can set a business apart from its competition. In markets with similar products and services, a guarantee can help clients make a decision. It communicates to potential buyers that the company stands behind its products and is dedicated to client happiness.

Developing long-term relationships

Customer trust is an essential component of long-term relationships. When firms provide and honor money-back guarantees, they exhibit dependability and integrity. This can lead to increased customer retention rates, since satisfied consumers are more inclined to return and make additional purchases.

Word of Mouth and Referrals

Customers who are satisfied with a company's money-back promise are more inclined to recommend it to others. Positive word-of-mouth and referrals can greatly improve a company's reputation and attract new clients.

Reducing Purchase Anxiety

Many customers feel anxious about making a purchase, especially when it comes to higher-priced items or new brands. A money-back guarantee can help ease this concern by acting as a safety net. Customers are more likely to make a purchase when they understand they may get their money back if they are dissatisfied.

Create a Money-Back Guarantee Policy
Understanding Your Market and Product.

Before creating a money-back guarantee policy, businesses should properly research their market and goods. This includes determining common customer problems, typical reasons for product returns, and the competitive landscape. By designing the guarantee to address these unique issues, businesses can develop a policy that appeals to their intended audience.

Clear and concise terms

An successful money-back guarantee policy should have simple and straightforward terms. Customers should understand what the guarantee covers, the conditions under which they can claim it, and how to request a return. Ambiguous or convoluted clauses can discourage customers from taking advantage of the promise, eroding trust.

Key Elements to Include

Duration: Determine the time limit during which customers can request a refund (e.g., 30 days, 60 days).

Conditions: Specify any requirements for the guarantee to apply.

Procedure: Describe the steps for seeking a refund, including contact information and any required paperwork or documentation.

Exclusions: Exclusions and limits should be clearly stated.

Easy Return Process

The process for claiming a money-back promise should be simple and painless. A difficult or time-consuming return process might undermine the benefits of the guarantee and annoy customers. Businesses should strive to make the return procedure as simple as possible, with a few steps and clear instructions.

Managing Returns and Refunds Effectively

Efficient handling of returns and refunds is critical for retaining consumer trust. Businesses should have mechanisms in place to handle returns and give refunds quickly. Delays or inaccuracies in processing can cause consumer unhappiness and harm the company's reputation.

Balancing Flexibility and Protection

While it is critical to provide a generous money-back guarantee to foster trust, businesses must also safeguard themselves against potential exploitation. Balancing client freedom with business protection is critical. Companies, for example, may set policies that limit the number of returns per consumer or require proof of purchase.

Communication of guarantees to customers
Prominent Display on Website and Marketing Materials

To make the most of a money-back promise, firms should prominently display it on their website and marketing materials. This includes displaying it on the homepage, product pages, checkout page, and adverts. Clear visibility ensures that potential clients are aware of the guarantee and feel reassured by its existence.

Clear and Honest Messaging

The messaging surrounding a money-back promise should be straightforward, honest, and transparent. Avoid using complex jargon or fine text that may confuse clients. Instead, utilize plain language to properly communicate the guarantee's important aspects.

Training Customer Service Teams

Customer care representatives should be properly taught on the money-back guarantee policy. They should be able to answer any questions that clients may have, walk them through the return process, and resolve refund requests efficiently. Providing customer care staff with the necessary expertise and tools can improve the entire client experience.

Leveraging Social Proof

Businesses can use social proof to boost the legitimacy of their money-back guarantees. This may include client testimonials, reviews, and case studies of satisfied customers who have successfully used the guarantee. Displaying these great stories can increase trust and inspire prospective customers to make a purchase.

Addressing Common Concerns

Common concerns about money-back guarantees should be addressed in the FAQ area of the website and other consumer interactions. This can include inquiries about the return process, refund timelines, and any special terms. Providing detailed responses can assist to manage consumer expectations and limit the frequency of requests.

Examples of Effective Money Back Guarantees
Case Study #1: Zappos

Background

Zappos, an online shoe and clothes shop, is known for its excellent customer service and generous return policy. The company has a 365-day money-back guarantee, which allows buyers to return things up to a year after purchase.

Key Features of Zappos' Guarantee

Duration: Zappos has a one-year return policy, which is much longer than the industry average.

No Questions Asked: No questions were asked. The guarantee is a "no questions asked" policy, which allows customers to return things for any reason.

Free Returns: Zappos offers free return postage, making the procedure even easier for customers.

Outcome

Zappos' money-back guarantee has helped to build its excellent brand recognition and customer loyalty. The liberal approach has reduced buying anxiety, encouraged repeat business, and established a high level of customer service in the sector.

Case Study #2: L.L. Bean

Background

L.L. Bean, a retailer that specializes in outdoor goods and equipment, is noted for its great guarantee. For many years, the company provided an unlimited return policy, which allowed customers to return things at any time.

Key Elements of the L.L. Bean Guarantee

Lifetime Guarantee: Historically, L.L. Bean's policy permitted returns for the life of the product.

Satisfaction Guaranteed: The guarantee was based on customer satisfaction, so customers could return things if they were dissatisfied.

Changes to Policy

L.L. Bean changed its return policy to a one-year period in 2018 in response to increased abuse. However, the corporation continues to accept returns for items with manufacturing flaws after the one-year period.

Outcome

Despite the changes, L.L. Bean's dedication to customer satisfaction and liberal return policy have kept customers trusting and loyal. The company's brand remains linked with quality and dependability.

Case Study #3: Warby Parker

Background

Warby Parker, an eyewear shop, provides a money-back guarantee as part of its home try-on program. Customers can trial five frames at home for free, with no commitment to buy.

Key Features of Warby Parker's Guarantee

Home Try-On: Customers can try out five frames at home for free for five days.

Free Returns: Customers can easily return the try-on frames because return postage is free.

30-Day Return Policy: Purchased frames include a 30-day return or exchange period.

Outcome

Warby Parker's money-back guarantee and home try-on program have made it easier for customers to buy glasses online. The risk-free trial lowered purchase anxiety and raised conversion rates, which aided the company's growth and success.

Case Study #4: Costco

Background

Costco, a membership warehouse club, provides a satisfaction guarantee on its products. The company's broad return policy applies to the majority of things offered in its outlets.

Key Features of Costco's Guarantee

Satisfaction Guarantee: Costco has a satisfaction guarantee, which allows consumers to return most items at any time if they are dissatisfied.

Electronics Return Policy: Costco provides a 90-day return policy on electronics from the date of purchase.

Membership Guarantee: If clients are dissatisfied with their membership, Costco will return their money at any time.

Outcome

Costco's satisfaction guarantee has resulted in significant customer loyalty and confidence. The company's dedication to standing by its products has boosted its reputation and promoted repeat business.

Case Study #5: Amazon

Background

Amazon, the world's largest online retailer, provides a money-back guarantee on a wide range of products sold through its site. The company's return policy differs based on the seller and product category, but it normally offers a dependable assurance to buyers.

Key Features of Amazon's Guarantee

30-Day Return Policy: Many things offered by Amazon have a 30-day return policy, which allows customers to return items within 30 days after receiving.

A-to-Z Guarantee: Amazon provides an A-to-Z Guarantee to third-party sellers, which protects buyers if things are not delivered on time, arrive damaged, or are not as advertised.

Easy Return Process: Amazon's return policy is intended to be straightforward and convenient, with options for prepaid return shipping labels and drop-off sites.

Outcome

Amazon's money-back guarantee and simple return policy have made it one of the most reputable internet businesses. The company's emphasis on client pleasure and convenience has fueled its expansion and maintained its market leadership.

Offering a money-back guarantee is an effective method for gaining consumer trust, increasing satisfaction, and distinguishing a company in a competitive marketplace. Businesses that provide a clear, fair, and easily accessible guarantee can minimize purchase anxiety, stimulate trial and repeat purchases, and foster long-term connections with their customers.

Understanding client expectations, setting clear and unambiguous terms, and assuring an easy return process are all necessary components of developing an effective money-back guarantee policy. The guarantee's impact can be enhanced further by effective communication through numerous channels and the use of social proof.helps the firm develop and succeed overall.

Zappos, L.L. Bean, Warby Parker, Costco, and Amazon all provide instances of how businesses can adopt successful money-back guarantees. These businesses have earned customer trust and loyalty by standing behind their products and prioritizing customer happiness.

In conclusion, a well-designed and clearly explained money-back guarantee may be a significant asset to any firm. It not only increases consumer confidence and contentment, but it also helps the firm develop and succeed overall

Chapter 9

Keeping an Eye on Trends

It is essential to be informed about industry trends and consumer behavior in the quickly changing business environment if you want to stay competitive and spur growth. Companies are better able to adjust their strategy, satisfy customer wants, and seize new possibilities when they comprehend and anticipate market changes. This chapter analyzes the value of trend monitoring, looks at several tools and techniques for trend analysis, and offers tips for modifying sales tactics to fit the needs of the market. It also includes case studies of businesses that have used trend knowledge to their advantage and seen notable commercial success.

The Value of Keeping Up with Market Trends and Purchase Behavior
Increasing Market Share

Companies that keep a close eye on market trends are better able to predict changes and modify their plans in time to stay ahead of the competition. Businesses can innovate and adapt faster than their rivals by keeping up with consumer tastes, market dynamics, and technological changes.

Fulfilling the Needs of Customers

Businesses may better align their products and services with customer expectations by having a deeper understanding of industry trends and buying habits. As a result of businesses' ability to provide solutions that adapt to changing demands and preferences, responsiveness promotes customer satisfaction and loyalty.

Finding Possibilities

By keeping an eye on trends, companies can find untapped markets and enhance their product offers. Early detection of market gaps or changing consumer wants might result in the creation of novel goods and services that boost sales.

Mitigation of Risk

Keeping up with industry developments aids businesses in recognizing possible hazards and difficulties. Businesses can create backup plans and strategies to lessen negative effects and ensure long-term stability and resilience by identifying hazards early.

Methodical Scheduling

For strategic planning and decision-making, trend analysis is vital. Trend monitoring can provide valuable insights that inform crucial corporate operations such as pricing models, marketing tactics, and product development. Long-term success and sustainable expansion are supported by this proactive strategy.

Equipment and Techniques for Trend Analysis

Market Analysis

Original investigation

Direct collection of original data from the source is the process of primary research. This approach offers personal knowledge about consumer preferences, behavior, and developing trends.

Questionnaires and surveys: These methods are useful for obtaining quantitative information from a broad audience and for gaining important insights into the preferences and purchasing patterns of consumers. Online platforms can be used by businesses to send surveys and effectively analyze the replies.

Focus groups: Focus groups entail a discussion of a product, service, or issue by small, diversified groups of consumers. Qualitative insights into the attitudes, motives, and perceptions of consumers are provided by this strategy.

Interviews: Detailed insights and viewpoints that surveys might miss can be uncovered through in-depth interviews with stakeholders, industry experts, and customers.

Observational research: Seeing how people behave in real-world situations, such online chat rooms or retail stores, can provide important details about their preferences and patterns of purchase.

Secondary Analysis

Analyzing material already in existence from a variety of sources is known as secondary research. This approach is economical and offers a thorough comprehension of market trends.

Industry Reports: Industry analysts, market research companies, and trade associations provide reports that provide in-depth analyses of consumer behavior, competitive environments, and market trends.

Scholarly Research: Scholarly investigations and writings offer comprehensive evaluations and conceptual models that can guide commercial tactics and trendspotting.

Competitor Analysis: Analyzing rivals' tactics, offerings, and market positioning can help identify new trends and changes in the sector. Companies can evaluate rivals by using techniques like SWOT analysis (Strengths, Weaknesses, Opportunities, and Threats).

Public statistics Sources: Reports and statistics that provide insightful information about market trends and economic conditions are frequently released by trade magazines, government agencies, and business associations.

Analysis of Sales Data

Understanding purchasing patterns and spotting trends require analyzing sales data. Sales data gives firms quantitative proof of customer behavior and preferences, enabling them to make well-informed decisions.

Sales statistics: Examining sales statistics on a regular basis enables companies to monitor performance, pinpoint best-selling items, and spot emerging trends or seasonal fluctuations.

CRM (customer relationship management) systems: CRMs gather and archive customer information, such as past purchases, preferences, and exchanges. Businesses can find trends in this data and adjust their plans by analyzing it.

Point-of-Sale (POS) Systems: By capturing transaction data in real-time, POS systems can shed light on product performance, peak shopping hours, and customer behavior.

Data analytics tools: To spot patterns, project demand, and improve inventory control, sophisticated analytics tools can analyze massive amounts of sales data.

Changing Sales Techniques in Response to Trends

Innovation in Product Design

Creating new goods and services to satisfy changing consumer demands is a common step in trend-following sales tactics. Trend analysis is a useful tool for businesses to find market gaps and create solutions to fill them.

Creating New Products: New product development that fits in with current trends can be guided by spotting market opportunities and growing consumer wants.

Enhancing Current items: Trend analysis can point up areas where current items could be made better, including by including more features, raising the standard of construction, or providing more customisation possibilities.

Promotion and Marketing

Businesses must modify their marketing and promotion methods in response to trends since they have a significant impact on consumer behavior and preferences.

Targeted Advertising: Businesses can develop more successful and focused advertising campaigns by better understanding their target audience through trend analysis.

Content marketing: By using trend analytics to inform content development, companies may create interesting and relevant content that appeals to their target audience.

Social Media Engagement: Keeping up with current trends on social media enables companies to interact with customers on well-known platforms and make use of hashtags and viral content.

Strategies for Pricing

Consumer price sensitivity and purchasing power can be impacted by trends. Companies should modify their pricing strategy to reflect the demands of the consumer and the state of the market.

Dynamic Pricing: By putting dynamic pricing models into practice, companies can modify their prices in response to current market conditions and demand.

Promotional Offers: Businesses can determine the ideal times to provide discounts, promotions, and exclusive deals in order to draw clients by analyzing patterns.

Channels of Distribution

Consumer preferences for channels of purchase, like mobile commerce, in-store experiences, and online buying, can be influenced by trends. To accommodate these demands, businesses should modify their distribution tactics.

E-Commerce Expansion: Businesses should make investments in strong e-commerce platforms and digital marketing tactics as the popularity of online shopping continues to rise.

Omnichannel Strategy: Using an omnichannel strategy guarantees that companies offer a unified and smooth buying experience through a variety of channels.

Case Studies of Companies That Respond to Trends
Case Study No. 1: Netflix

Context

Leading streaming provider Netflix has proven to be incredibly sensitive to changes in the market and in customer behavior. Netflix made the switch from DVD rentals to online streaming by taking advantage of new developments in the consumption of digital media.

Adapting to Trends

Change to Streaming: Netflix made the switch from renting out DVDs to providing streaming services after realizing the popularity of online content consumption. The business was able to penetrate the growing digital entertainment market thanks to this calculated approach.

Original material: In response to the trend of consumers seeking for exclusive and superior material, Netflix made significant investments in the creation of original content. Television programs such as "Stranger Things" and "The Crown" have fostered brand loyalty and subscriber growth.

Data-Driven Decisions: Netflix makes predictions about trends and understands viewer preferences by using data analytics. Marketing strategies, tailored recommendations, and content development are all influenced by this data-driven methodology.

Result

Netflix has become a dominant force in the streaming market thanks to its ability to adapt to market changes and drive its growth. The company has seen a significant gain in subscribers and market share as a result of its ability to adjust to shifting consumer behavior and invest in unique content.

Apple in Case Study No. 2

Context

Leading the way in technology worldwide, Apple is renowned for its cutting-edge goods and avant-garde business practices. To keep ahead of the competition, the organization continuously tracks consumer preferences and industry developments.

Adapting to Trends

Smartphone Revolution: By releasing the iPhone, Apple was able to take advantage of the expanding trend of mobile communication. The iPhone transformed the smartphone market and raised the bar for usefulness and design.

Wearable Technology: Apple created the Apple Watch after observing the trend toward fitness and wellness.

With features like health tracking, notifications, and compatibility with other Apple devices, this product has emerged as a pioneer in the wearable technology industry.

Service Expansion: In response to the rise of digital content consumption and subscription-based business models, Apple has increased the number of services it offers, such as Apple Music, Apple TV+, and Apple Arcade.

Result

Apple's dominance of the market has been cemented by its capacity to recognize and adapt to trends. The company is among the most valuable in the world because to its cutting-edge goods and services, which have significantly increased revenue and increased brand loyalty.

Third Case Study: Starbucks

Context

The international chain of Starbucks coffee shops has proven to be adept at adjusting to shifting consumer tastes and market trends. To remain current, the business constantly updates its products and clientele's experience.

Adapting to Trends

Mobile Ordering and Payment: Starbucks launched a mobile app that enables consumers to place orders and make payments in advance in response to the rise of mobile technology and convenience. This invention has simplified processes and improved client convenience.

Health and Wellness: In response to the growing trend of consumers becoming more health-conscious, Starbucks has added healthier options to its menu, including salads, plant-based beverages, and protein boxes.

Sustainability: Starbucks has introduced programs including recyclable cups, a reduction in the use of plastic, and the procurement of coffee that is produced ethically in response to the movement toward environmental sustainability.

Result

Starbucks' brand and consumer devotion have become stronger as a result of its ability to adjust to changes. Customers have responded favorably to the company's emphasis on innovation, health, and sustainability, which has aided in its sustained growth and international expansion.

Tesla Case Study No. 4

Context

The maker of electric vehicles (EVs), Tesla, has profited greatly from new developments in sustainable transportation and renewable energy. The business has established itself as a leader in the automobile sector because to its trend-responsive methods.

Adapting to Trends

Electric Vehicles: Tesla was the first to produce high-performance electric vehicles after realizing the need for environmentally friendly transportation. Due to the company's emphasis on EV technology, there has been a notable increase in consumer interest and market uptake.

Autonomous Driving: Tesla has made significant investments in the development of cutting-edge driver-assistance and self-driving technologies in response to the trend of autonomous vehicles. Tesla is now a market leader for autonomous vehicles thanks to this breakthrough.

Renewable Energy: Solar panels and energy storage systems are examples of the renewable energy solutions that Tesla has added to its lineup. This diversification is in line with the movement toward sustainable living and the use of renewable energy.

Result

Tesla's quick rise to the top of the market has been propelled by its adaptability to developments in renewable energy and environmentally friendly transportation. The company has drawn a sizable investor base and a devoted client base because to its inventive goods and forward-thinking business practices.

In summary, for firms to remain competitive, satisfy client wants, and spot new opportunities, trend monitoring is crucial. Businesses can modify their sales tactics and spur expansion by utilizing trend-responsive techniques, sales data analysis, and market research. The Netflix, Apple, Starbucks, and Tesla case studies highlight the value of keeping abreast of market developments and the possibility of substantial economic success through proactive adaptation. An organization can set itself up for long-term growth and success by embracing trend analysis and continuously adjusting to match shifting market conditions.

Chapter 10

Making Use of Technology

In the current digital world, using technology to improve client connections, streamline sales processes, and spur revenue growth has become essential. Technology makes it possible for sales teams to operate more productively and efficiently, from Customer Relationship Management (CRM) systems to sophisticated data analytics and sales automation technologies. This chapter examines the several technologies, such as data analytics, sales automation, and CRM systems, that can be used to enhance sales performance. It also offers instances of how top businesses have successfully used technology into their sales methods.

Utilizing CRM Programs

A CRM System: What Is It?

A software platform called a Customer Relationship Management (CRM) system is made to help businesses better manage their relationships with both present and potential clients. It improves the capacity to manage and evaluate client interactions throughout the sales cycle, centralizes customer data, and simplifies communication.

Increased Efficiency and Productivity

CRM systems automate many routine tasks, such as data entry, follow-up reminders, and reporting. This automation frees up time for sales representatives to focus on more strategic activities, such as engaging with prospects and closing deals.

Better Sales Tracking and Forecasting

CRM systems provide real-time insights into sales performance, allowing managers to track progress against targets, identify bottlenecks, and forecast future sales. These insights enable more informed decision-making and strategic planning.

Enhanced Productivity and Efficiency

Numerous repetitive processes, including data entry, follow-up reminders, and reporting, are automated by CRM systems. Salespeople may now devote more of their time to more strategic tasks, including interacting with prospects and completing deals, thanks to this automation.

Improved Forecasting and Tracking of Sales

CRM systems give managers instantaneous insights into sales performance, enabling them to monitor progress toward goals, spot bottlenecks, and project future sales. Strategic planning and decision-making are made possible by these insights.

Important CRM System Features

Management of Contacts

CRM systems keep track of extensive data about clients and potential clients, such as contact information, correspondence records, and demographic data. Sales teams will always have a comprehensive picture of their clientele thanks to this functionality.

Sales Pipeline Management

CRM systems allow sales teams to follow the movement of leads through the sales pipeline, from initial contact to completing the purchase. This visibility helps sales personnel prioritize their efforts and discover possibilities that demand quick attention.

Lead Management

CRM systems enable sales teams capture, track, and nurture leads. By automating lead scoring and qualification processes, CRM systems ensure that sales personnel focus on the most promising opportunities.

Reporting and Analytics

CRM systems give customisable reports and dashboards that offer insights into sales performance, customer behavior, and market trends. These analytics assist sales teams discover strengths and weaknesses and make data-driven decisions.

Examples of CRM Systems

Salesforce

Salesforce is one of the most extensively used CRM platforms, delivering a range of functions for sales, marketing, and customer service. It provides extensive capabilities for managing client connections, automating sales processes, and evaluating data.

HubSpot

HubSpot CRM is noted for its user-friendly interface and integration with HubSpot's marketing and support solutions. It features contact management, sales pipeline tracking, and sophisticated reporting tools, making it a popular choice for small to mid-sized organizations.

Zoho CRM

Zoho CRM offers a scalable and adaptable platform with capabilities such as lead management, sales automation, and advanced analytics. It connects with numerous third-party programs, offering a seamless workflow for sales teams.

Automation in Sales Processes

What is Sales Automation?

Sales automation refers to the use of technology to automate repetitive and time-consuming processes within the sales process. This automation helps sales teams operate more effectively, decrease errors, and focus on high-value activities that drive revenue.

Benefits of Sales Automation

Increased Efficiency

By automating typical processes like as data entry, follow-up emails, and scheduling, sales automation decreases the administrative burden on sales professionals. This increased productivity allows them to spend more time engaging with customers and closing agreements.

Improved Accuracy

Sales automation decreases the possibility of human mistake in tasks such as data entry and lead assessment. Accurate and consistent data ensures that sales teams make informed judgments and maintain dependable records.

Enhanced Lead Nurturing

Sales automation offers targeted and timely connection with leads. Automated workflows can send personalized emails, follow-up reminders, and content based on the lead's behavior and stage in the sales funnel, enhancing lead nurturing and conversion rates.

Simplified Procedures for Sales

By standardizing sales procedures, sales automation makes sure that everyone in the team abides by the rules and best practices. The sales process becomes more predictable and consistent as a result of this standardization.

Important Elements of Sales Automation

Automated Emails

Sales teams can send targeted and tailored emails at scale with email automation. Based on predetermined triggers, automated email sequences can re-engage inactive clients, nurture leads, and follow up with prospects.

Lead Point Calculation

With automated lead scoring, every lead is given a number depending on how they behave and engage with the business. Salespeople can more effectively prioritize their efforts and concentrate on leads that have the best chance of converting by using this grading system.

Automation of Tasks

Tools for automating tasks Set up and remind sales reps of follow-up calls, meetings, and email outreach, among other crucial tasks. This automation guarantees that sales activities are finished on schedule and that no opportunities are lost.

Sales Information

Real-time insights into lead activity, pipeline health, and sales effectiveness are available through automated sales analytics. Sales teams may analyze progress, spot trends, and make data-driven decisions with the aid of these insights.

Tools for Sales Automation Examples

Salesloft

A sales engagement tool called Salesloft automates lead follow-up, call scheduling, and email marketing. It offers resources for tracking lead engagements, customizing email sequences, and evaluating sales results.

Reach-out

With the help of task reminders, analytics, and automated email sequences, sales teams may interact with prospects by using Outreach, a sales automation tool. It may be integrated with CRM systems to improve sales efficiency and offer a smooth workflow.

Pipedriver

Sales teams can track deals, manage leads, and automate repetitive processes using Pipedrive, a sales CRM and automation platform. It provides capabilities for sales reporting, email automation, and configurable pipelines.

Analytics of Data for Sales Perspectives

Data Analytics's Significance in Sales

Because data analytics offers practical insights into customer behavior, sales performance, and market trends, it is essential to contemporary sales strategy. Sales teams may increase revenue, streamline operations, and make well-informed decisions by utilizing data analytics.

The advantages of data analytics

Improving Decision-Making

Sales teams can obtain comprehensive insights into market dynamics, consumer preferences, and sales performance through data analytics. Strategic planning and decision-making are made possible by these insights.

Enhanced comprehension of customers

Sales teams can spot patterns and trends in customer behavior by examining customer data. This knowledge facilitates more individualized interactions, more tailored sales strategies, and more client satisfaction.

Enhanced Sales Procedures

In the sales process, data analytics is useful in locating inefficiencies and bottlenecks. Sales teams can take remedial action to expedite processes and increase conversion rates by identifying the location and reason behind blocked deals.

Forecasting Understandings

Utilizing past data, predictive analytics makes predictions about future customer behavior and sales success. Sales teams may use these information to plan ahead, allocate resources wisely, and create proactive tactics.

Important Domains in Sales Data Analytics
Analysis of Sales Performance

Finding the best-performing items, salespeople, and marketing channels is made easier by analyzing sales performance data. This analysis sheds light on the factors influencing sales success and the areas in need of development.

Client Division

Based on their characteristics, preferences, and behavior, the client base is divided into discrete groups through customer segmentation. Sales teams can customize their strategies and develop niche marketing campaigns for every segment thanks to this segmentation.

Analysis of Leads and Opportunities

Sales teams can better evaluate the efficacy of their lead generation and conversion tactics by analyzing lead and opportunity data. High-potential leads, effective lead sources, and regions in the sales funnel that need to be improved are all identified by this research.

Analyzing Pipelines

The sales pipeline's condition and development can be understood through pipeline analysis. Through the monitoring of crucial indicators like transaction velocity, win/loss ratios, and conversion rates, sales teams may pinpoint obstacles and enhance the efficiency of their approach.

Tools for Data Analytics Examples

Tableau

Sales teams may analyze and present data in a visually appealing and dynamic manner with the aid of Tableau, an analytics and data visualization platform. It provides comprehensive analytics features, customized dashboards, and drag-and-drop flexibility.

Power BI for Microsoft

A business analytics application called Microsoft Power BI helps sales teams to communicate, display, and share data insights. It provides real-time analytics, interactive reports, and strong data integration capabilities.

Google Data

A web analytics program called Google Analytics may tell you about user behavior, website traffic, and marketing effectiveness. It assists sales teams in optimizing digital strategies and comprehending the efficacy of online marketing initiatives.

Examples of Sales Strategies Enhanced by Technology
First Case Study: Salesforce

Context

Salesforce, a leading provider of CRM solutions worldwide, has effectively incorporated technology to improve its sales tactics and stimulate revenue expansion.

Methodology

All-Inclusive CRM Platform: Salesforce offers real-time insights into sales success, centralizes customer data, and simplifies communication. Sales teams can better manage their customer interactions with the help of this technology.

Sales Automation: Salesforce automates regular processes like data entry, follow-up emails, and reporting in sales. By increasing efficiency, this automation frees up sales personnel to concentrate on high-value tasks.

Advanced Analytics: Salesforce leverages data analytics to understand market trends, sales performance, and customer behavior. These insights assist in streamlining sales procedures and informing strategic decisions.

Result

Salesforce's quick expansion and dominant position in the market are partly attributable to its technologically advanced sales tactics. Strong client relationships and significant revenue generation have been made possible by the company's CRM platform and superior analytics capabilities.

Case Study No. 2: Amazon

Context

The biggest online retailer in the world, Amazon, has improved consumer experiences and streamlined sales processes by utilizing technology.

Methodology

CRM Integration: By centralizing customer data, Amazon's CRM system offers a thorough insight of each customer's preferences and past purchases. Amazon is able to increase customer happiness and personalize suggestions because to this connectivity.

Sales Automation: To expedite order processing, inventory control, and customer communication, Amazon uses automation solutions. This automation guarantees a flawless shopping experience while boosting efficiency.

Data Analytics: Amazon uses data analytics to track sales success, examine consumer behavior, and spot market trends. Amazon uses these insights to improve its marketing campaigns, price policies, and product offerings.

Result

Amazon's quick expansion and market dominance can be attributed to its technology-enhanced sales techniques. The organization has generated substantial income and provided outstanding customer experiences by utilizing data analytics, sales automation, and CRM integration.

Microsoft Case Study No. 3

Context

Leading global technology company Microsoft has effectively incorporated technology-enhanced sales techniques to boost income and strengthen client relationships.

Methodology

CRM Platform: Microsoft manages customer interactions, automates sales processes, and conducts data analysis using Dynamics 365, its own CRM platform. A consolidated view of client interactions and sales performance is offered by this platform.

Sales Automation: Microsoft automates regular processes like lead scoring, follow-up emails, and reporting in the sales domain. By increasing efficiency, this automation frees up sales personnel to concentrate on more critical tasks.

Data Analytics: Microsoft uses data analytics and advanced analytics to understand market trends, sales performance, and customer behavior. These insights assist in streamlining sales procedures and informing strategic decisions.

Result

Microsoft's success and market supremacy can be attributed to its technology-enhanced sales methods. The organization has been able to generate substantial revenue and cultivate strong client connections through the implementation of CRM, sales automation, and data analytics.

Chapter 11

Education and Training

Continuous training and development are essential for keeping a competitive edge and promoting steady revenue growth in the quickly changing sales environment. To efficiently fulfill customer needs and surpass sales targets, sales teams need to be well-equipped with the newest product knowledge, sales strategies, and customer service abilities. This chapter examines the value of continuous sales training, the main areas that training initiatives should concentrate on, and strategies for providing sales teams with efficient training.

The Value of Constant Sales Education
Changing with the Market

Technology developments, consumer behavior, and market dynamics all have an ongoing impact on the corporate environment. Constant sales training keeps sales teams abreast of the newest techniques, technologies, and best practices, allowing them to adjust to changes fast and continue to be productive.

Improving Understanding of the Product

For salespeople to properly convey the characteristics and benefits of their goods or services, they must possess in-depth product expertise. Sales personnel may deliver accurate and convincing information to customers by staying up to date on industry standards, new product developments, and features through ongoing training.

Enhancing Methods of Selling

Strategies and tactics for sales change with time. Frequent training assists sales teams in developing new techniques, honing existing ones, and implementing creative selling strategies. Their capacity to interact with prospects, handle objections, and close agreements is improved by this ongoing progress.

Increasing Contentment with Clients

The key to long-term success and repeat business is satisfied customers. Training courses that concentrate on customer service techniques assist sales teams in strengthening their bonds with clients, successfully resolving their issues, and providing outstanding service. Customers that are happy with a brand are more inclined to stick with it and refer others to it.

Boosting Retention and Employee Motivation

Putting money into the training of sales staff shows that you care about their success and professional development. Increased motivation, decreased turnover rates, and more job satisfaction can all result from this investment. Workers are more likely to stick with the company and contribute to its long-term success if they feel appreciated and supported.

Focus Areas for Training Initiatives
Product Understanding

Recognizing Benefits and Features: Teams in charge of sales need to be extremely knowledgeable about the goods and services they are marketing. Training courses ought to go over each offering's salient characteristics, advantages, and differentiators. Salespeople can effectively convey to customers the value of their products and set themselves apart from competitors with the use of this information.

Keeping Up with Updates for Products: Product offerings are subject to continuous changes due to the regular introduction of new features, versions, and enhancements. Constant training guarantees that sales personnel have access to the most recent product information, allowing them to give customers accurate and pertinent information.

Knowledge of the Industry: Sales personnel should be well-versed in industry trends, standards, and laws in addition to product-specific expertise. Sales personnel can more successfully position their products and handle any customer concerns particular to the sector by having a better understanding of the larger industry environment.

Strategies for Selling

Advisory Sales: Building relationships with clients and learning about their needs before presenting a solution is the main goal of consultative selling. Sales staff should learn how to listen intently, pose thoughtful questions, and modify their strategy to fit the unique demands of each client through training programs.

Offering Solutions: Finding a customer's pain spots and offering a good or service as the perfect answer to their issue is known as solution selling. Techniques for identifying customer problems, showcasing the benefits of the solution, and clearly communicating how the product solves the customer's problems should all be included in sales training.

Skills in Negotiation: Proficiency in negotiation is vital in finalizing agreements and attaining advantageous results for the client and the business. Sales staff should learn how to deal with objections, negotiate terms, and come to mutually beneficial agreements from training programs.

Closing Methods: For any sales professional, closing deals is an essential talent. Different closing strategies, including the assumptive close, the urgency close, and the alternate choice close, should be covered in training. Sales staff should become adept at spotting buying cues so they can approach a customer with confidence.

Client Support

Establishing rapport: Establishing rapport with clients is essential to establishing long-term partnerships and earning their trust. Techniques for building a friendly and professional relationship with consumers, demonstrating empathy, and connecting with them should be the main focus of training programs.

Successful Interaction: Understanding client needs and communicating product information require clear and effective communication. Training in verbal and textual communication techniques, such as active listening, benefit clarification, and handling client issues, should be provided to sales staff.

Managing Complicated Clients: Patience, tact, and problem-solving abilities are necessary while dealing with challenging clients. Sales personnel should be given the tools they need through training programs to handle difficult situations, defuse tension, and turn bad experiences around.

After-Sale Assistance: After the sale, customer support doesn't stop. Delivering first-rate after-sale service is essential to keeping customers happy and satisfied. Best practices for following up with clients, handling problems that arise after a sale, and making sure they are happy with their purchase should all be included in training.

Techniques for Providing Training Effectively

Personal Instruction

Workshops and Seminars: Interactive and immersive training is offered through workshops and seminars. These seminars can go into great detail on particular subjects and provide sales teams the chance to participate in role-playing games, group discussions, and practical activities. In-person instruction improves learning by encouraging teamwork and quick feedback.

On-the-Job Training: In this type of training, rookie sales representatives observe more seasoned colleagues and take part in actual sales tasks in order to learn by doing. With the help of this approach, students can apply their knowledge in a safe and encouraging atmosphere while gaining real-world experience.

Online Education

E-learning Modules: Sales personnel may complete training at their own pace and from any location with the flexibility and accessibility that e-learning modules provide. To support learning, these modules may contain interactive material, tests, and assessments. Offering standardized training to teams who are spread out geographically can be accomplished efficiently with e-learning.

Webinars: Webinars are online sessions, either live or recorded, that address particular training subjects. They provide the option for participation from a distance and may incorporate interactive features like surveys and

Q&A sessions. A cheap method of simultaneously providing training to big numbers of participants is through webinars.

Blended Learning

Integrating Online and In-Person Instruction: The advantages of both online and in-person training are combined in blended learning. This method offers a thorough training experience, combining the personal interaction and interactive nature of in-person sessions with the flexibility of online courses. Training programs can be more effectively and specifically personalized with blended learning.

Mentorship Programs: These programs match aspiring sales reps with seasoned mentors who offer advice, encouragement, and constructive criticism. Because of this relationship, which promotes lifelong learning and professional growth, mentees can pick up insightful knowledge and useful skills from their mentors.

Gamification

Interactive Learning: To boost motivation and engagement, interactive learning programs can be gamified by adding game components. Quizzes, role-playing, and competitions are examples of interactive learning activities that enhance training enjoyment and promote active participation.

Incentives and prizes: Sales staff can be encouraged to interact with training content by providing incentives and prizes for finishing training modules and hitting learning objectives. Acknowledging and praising success promotes a healthy learning environment and constant progress.

Role-playing and Case Studies

Real-World Scenarios: Sales teams can use case studies to examine real-world situations and use their expertise to resolve issues. Talking about case studies enables students to absorb real-world experiences and comprehend how their instruction is applied practically.

Role-playing exercises: By simulating sales encounters, role-playing exercises give learners a safe setting in which to hone their skills. Through these exercises, sales teams can improve their methods, gain self-assurance, and get helpful criticism from trainers and their peers.

Instances of Successful Training Initiatives

Sales Academy at IBM

Summary: IBM Sales Academy is a thorough training program created to advance the abilities and expertise of IBM sales representatives. The course covers a variety of sales-related topics, such as customer service, sales tactics, and product expertise.

Methods of Training: Watson Sales Academy employs a blended learning strategy that mixes online courses, in-person seminars, and mentorship initiatives. In addition to case study discussions and role-playing activities, trainees take part in interactive workshops. In order to increase participation, the program also includes gamification components.

Results: IBM Sales Academy alumni report better sales techniques, more self-assurance, and a deeper comprehension of IBM's offerings. Across the board, the approach has improved customer happiness and sales success.

HubSpot Sales Education

Overview: To give sales teams the tools they need to succeed in inbound sales, HubSpot provides a thorough sales training curriculum. Consultative selling, lead nurturing, and effective communication are the program's main focuses.

Training Methods: Live webinars, interactive workshops, and e-learning modules are all part of HubSpot's training curriculum. In addition, the application gives users access to a resource library that contains best practices, instructions, and templates. Sales teams can take part in role-playing games and get input from knowledgeable trainers.

Results: HubSpot's sales training program participants report better client interactions, increased lead conversion rates, and improved sales skills. HubSpot's sales teams now better align with the company's inbound sales process thanks to the program.

Google Sales Expertise

Overview: Google's sales professionals are the target audience for Google Sales Mastery, an advanced training program. Deep product knowledge, sophisticated sales strategies, and strategic client connection abilities are the main goals of the curriculum.

Training Methods: Online courses, mentorship programs, and in-person training sessions are all used by Google Sales Mastery. Role-playing exercises, real-world case studies, and interactive seminars are all included in the program. Sales teams can take use of an extensive knowledge base and continuous assistance from seasoned mentors.

Results: Graduates of Google Sales Mastery exhibit a high degree of product and service knowledge. A more strategic approach to sales, improved client connections, and higher sales performance have all resulted from the program.

In summary, for sales teams to maintain their competitiveness, adjust to shifting market conditions, and see steady revenue growth, they must engage in ongoing training and development. Good training programs use a range of delivery modalities, including as in-person instruction, online modules, and blended learning strategies, and concentrate on important topics like product knowledge, sales strategies, and customer service. Businesses can boost customer happiness, staff motivation, and long-term business success by investing in the ongoing development of their sales teams. Successful training initiatives have a major impact on sales performance and the overall success of an organization, as demonstrated by the cases of IBM, HubSpot, and Google.

Chapter 12

Establishing Robust Connections

The key to success in sales is developing solid relationships. The ability to establish and sustain meaningful connections with consumers is frequently what distinguishes great sales professionals, even while product knowledge and sales strategies are important. This chapter examines the value of developing connections with customers, strategies for doing so, and case examples that highlight effective relationship-building tactics.

The Value of Developing Relationships in Sales

Building Trust: Any effective sales connection is built on trust. Consumers who trust and feel at ease with a salesperson are more likely to make a purchase from them. Sales professionals may create trust with their customers and increase the likelihood that they will become repeat customers by cultivating good connections.

Boosting Customer Loyalty: Strong bonds with customers result in a rise in their loyalty. Customers are more inclined to make repeat purchases and refer the company to others when they feel appreciated and understood. In addition to bringing in repeat business, loyal consumers work as brand ambassadors, boosting the business's visibility and drawing in new customers.

Improving Customer contentment: A customer's contentment can be greatly increased by having a good relationship with a salesperson. Customers are more likely to have a favorable experience when they believe their demands are understood and that their issues are immediately addressed. Positive word-of-mouth advertising and increased retention rates can result from this contentment.

Encouraging Upselling and Cross-Selling: Salespeople can better understand the needs and preferences of their clients by developing close connections with them. This knowledge facilitates the identification of upselling and cross-selling opportunities, which provide value for the customer and boost revenue for the company.

Increasing Sales Performance: Salespeople who are adept at fostering relationships frequently have higher sales results. Longer engagement times, bigger transactions, and more recommendations are all possible outcomes of strong connections. Salespeople can develop a steady stream of possibilities by devoting time and energy to cultivating relationships.

Methods for Developing Stronger Customer Connections
Frequent Check-Ins

The Value of Remainders

Consistent follow-ups show clients that you appreciate and cherish them. Following up with customers following a meeting, sale, or customer service encounter demonstrates the salesperson's dedication to guaranteeing client happiness and taking care of any lingering issues.

Techniques for Monitoring

Emails: A good strategy to stay in touch with customers is to send them customized follow-up emails. These emails may offer special deals, details on new products, or just a quick hello to see how the consumer is doing.

Calls: A follow-up call enables more engaging contact and can provide a personal touch. This approach is very helpful for answering any queries or concerns the client may have.

Thank-You Notes: Expressing sincere gratitude for a customer's business with a handwritten message following a transaction or meeting can make a lasting impression.

Surveys: Asking customers about their experiences and demonstrating that the salesperson values their input can both be accomplished by sending them a follow-up survey.

When to Follow Up

When to follow up is really important. After a meeting or transaction, following up right away helps strengthen the relationship; but, following up on a regular basis can help it last. Finding the right balance between being in contact and not bothering the customer too much is crucial.

Customized Wording

Recognizing Client Preferences

Customizing communications to a customer's tastes, interests, and behaviors is known as personalized communication. To provide a more customized experience, salespeople should take the time to learn about the particular requirements and preferences of each client.

Methods of Customization

Addressing Customers by Name: Using the customer's name when communicating with them might make the exchange more intimate and lively.

Customized Messages: You can increase the relevance and significance of your communication by adjusting it based on the customer's past interactions or special interests.

Recalling Crucial Information: A salesperson can demonstrate that they are paying attention and are concerned about their customer by recalling and bringing up information about their preferences, previous transactions, or significant occasions (like birthdays).

Making Relevant Recommendations: Making recommendations for goods or services based on a customer's past purchases or declared interests can improve customer satisfaction and show a personalized approach.

Instruments for Customization

CRM (Customer Relationship Management) Systems: CRMs facilitate the personalization of sales interactions by storing comprehensive customer information.

Email marketing platforms: These platforms frequently come with personalization options like dynamic content that adapts to the profile of the recipient.

Social Media: Interacting with clients on social media platforms can yield valuable information about their preferences and areas of interest, facilitating more tailored exchanges.

Case Studies of Effective Relationship Development
Case 1: Zappos

Context

Online shoe and apparel store Zappos is well-known for its strong client relationships and outstanding customer service. The company's success can be attributed in large part to its dedication to fostering relationships.

Methods

Personalized Service: Zappos encourages its customer care agents to spend time getting to know each individual client's requirements in order to make recommendations that are specifically tailored to them.

Frequent Follow-Ups: The business follows up with clients to find out if they are happy with their purchases and to quickly resolve any concerns.

Employee Empowerment: Zappos gives its staff members the freedom to go above and above for clients, for as by delivering unexpected presents and handwritten messages of gratitude.

Result

Zappos has a devoted client base and a solid reputation for customer service as a result of their emphasis on developing relationships. The company's sustained success and expansion may be attributed to its unwavering commitment to delivering exceptional customer experiences.

Case Study No. 2: Nordstrom

Context

The upscale department store Nordstrom is renowned for its outstanding customer service and dedication to fostering long-lasting relationships with its patrons.

Methods

Personalized Shopping Experience: Personal stylists at Nordstrom provide recommendations that are specifically catered to the preferences of their clients.

Follow-Up: Following a customer's purchase, the business contacts them again to make sure they're satisfied and to extend an offer of help.

Customer Appreciation Events: To foster relationships and express gratitude for their business, Nordstrom organizes special events for its most devoted patrons.

Result

Due to Nordstrom's emphasis on individualized care and frequent follow-ups, client satisfaction has increased and the company has developed a devoted following. The company's success and stellar reputation are largely attributable to its relationship-building initiatives.

Salesforce in Case Study No. 3

Context

One of the top platforms for customer relationship management (CRM), Salesforce, places a premium on fostering close bonds with its clients.

Methods

Customer Success Managers: To assist clients in reaching their objectives and optimizing the platform's value, Salesforce designates specialized customer success managers.

Frequent Check-Ins: The business checks in with clients on a regular basis to handle any issues, give updates, and provide assistance.

Customized Solutions: Salesforce offers customized solutions that are based on the unique requirements and goals of every client, guaranteeing a customized experience.

Result

Salesforce's dedication to fostering great relationships and achieving client success has led to high rates of customer satisfaction and retention. The company's development and leadership in the CRM business can be attributed to its customized strategy.

Conclusion

Success in sales requires the development of solid relationships. Meaningful relationships between salespeople and customers improve trust, loyalty, and customer happiness. Nurturing these relationships requires the use of strategies like tailored communication and frequent follow-ups. Empirical evidence from corporations such as Zappos, Nordstrom, and Salesforce demonstrates the noteworthy influence of proficient relationship-building strategies on enduring economic prosperity.

Putting money into relationship-building initiatives not only boosts sales results but also lays the groundwork for future expansion. Salespeople can create enduring connections that encourage repeat business, produce referrals, and enhance the company's success overall by getting to know and value each individual customer.

Chapter 13

Establishing and Reaching Sales Objectives

Any business's capacity to generate revenue and maintain growth and sustainability depends on its ability to set and meet sales targets. Sales teams are given direction, focus, and incentive by having sales goals that are clear, reasonable, and attainable. This helps to match their efforts with the company's larger aims. This chapter examines the significance of well-defined sales objectives, techniques for establishing reasonable and attainable goals, and approaches for inspiring and monitoring team performance.

Clear Sales Objectives Are Essential
Giving Guidance and Attention: Teams can clearly focus and have a direction when they have sales targets. They give an overview of the goals to be met as well as a path forward. Without specific objectives, sales efforts may become dispersed and ineffective, which could result in poor performance and lost opportunities.

Aligning with Business Objectives: The sales team's activities are coordinated with the company's overarching goals when they have well-defined sales targets. Reaching corporate objectives and advancing the broader business plan are aided by this connection. It guarantees that each and every sales action advances the goals and objectives of the business.

Measuring Performance: The standard by which performance is measured is sales targets. They make it possible for sales managers to monitor advancement, pinpoint areas in need of development, and honor top workers. Businesses can assess their plans and make data-driven decisions by contrasting actual results with predetermined targets.

Creating Well-Defined Sales Goals: Sales teams can be highly motivated by clearly-defined goals. They offer a purpose and a well-defined goal to strive toward. Reaching these objectives can result in praise, incentives, and a feeling of achievement, which can improve morale and motivate ongoing work.

Encouraging Accountability: Clearly defined sales objectives help the sales team to be accountable. Members of a team who are aware of their individual and group goals are more likely to take responsibility for their work and make an effort to either reach or surpass expectations.

Techniques for Creating Achievable and Realistic Goals
SMART Objectives

Definition

The words "specific, measurable, achievable, relevant, and time-bound" are abbreviated as "SMART." Sales targets that are SMART (specific, attainable, reasonable, and time-bound) are guaranteed.

Components Specific: Objectives must to be precise and unambiguous, defining the precise expectations. An explicit goal might be to "increase sales of Product X by 10% in the next quarter," as opposed to just "increase sales."

Measurable: In order to monitor progress, goals must be quantifiable. This entails establishing benchmarks for tracking development and figuring out when the objective has been met. A measurable aim, such as "increase sales of Product X by 10%," is one that can be quantified.

Achievable: Objectives must to be reachable and reasonable. They ought to push the sales staff while staying within the bounds of possibility. If too lofty ambitions are thought to be unachievable, they may demotivate you.

Relevant: Objectives ought to be pertinent to the overarching corporate goals. They ought to support the company's long-term performance and be in line with its plan. Increasing the sales of a high-margin product, for instance, can be more pertinent than concentrating on a low-margin item.

Time-bound: Objectives ought to have a specified end date. This makes things seem more urgent and facilitates planning and task prioritization. For instance, because it outlines a three-month period, the goal "increase sales of Product X by 10% in the next quarter" is time-bound.

KPIs, or key performance indicators

Definition

Measurable values known as Key Performance Indicators (KPIs) show how well a business is accomplishing its main goals. KPIs offer a means to gauge the effectiveness of sales initiatives and monitor advancement toward sales targets in the context of sales.

Typical Sales KPIs
Revenue Growth: Calculates the rise in sales income over a given time frame. It shows how well sales efforts have performed overall.

Sales Target Achievement: Sales Target Tracks the proportion of sales targets that are either fulfilled or surpassed. It aids in determining how successful sales tactics are.

Customer Acquisition Cost (CAC): The expense of obtaining a new customer is measured by the Customer Acquisition expense (CAC). More effective sales procedures are indicated by a lower CAC.

Customer Lifetime Value (CLV): Customer Lifetime Value (CLV) is a measure of how much money a company can make from a single customer over the course of that customer's relationship. A higher CLV indicates that upselling and customer retention tactics are working.

Conversion Rate: Monitors the proportion of leads that become paying clients. Increased conversion rates are a sign of successful sales strategies.

Average Deal Size: Calculates the mean amount of money that is sold. It aids in comprehending how profitable sales endeavors are.

Sales Cycle Length: Measures the typical amount of time needed to complete a sale. More effective sales procedures are indicated by shorter sales cycles.

As an illustration

A KPI for a sales team could be: "Achieve a 20% conversion rate for leads generated through online marketing campaigns" could be a sales team's key performance indicator.

Choosing Reasonable Goals

Examining Past Information

Analyzing previous sales data is necessary to set reasonable sales targets. This entails looking back at previous results, seeing patterns, and knowing what was feasible in earlier times. Past performance serves as a standard for establishing new objectives.

Taking the Market Conditions into Account

Realistic sales targets are largely dependent on the state of the market. This covers elements including the competitive environment, industry trends, and economic situations. It is easier to set realistic goals that take into account the current state of the market when one is aware of these conditions.

Including the Sales Staff

Setting goals with the sales team in mind can result in more achievable and realistic objectives. Salespeople are intimately familiar with the demands, difficulties, and opportunities of their clients. Their opinions can offer insightful information and support in establishing goals that are both challenging and doable.

Establishing Gradual Objectives

Achieving long-term goals can be facilitated by setting incremental targets. Larger goals can be broken down into smaller, more achievable aims, allowing for slow development and frequent opportunity for evaluation and modification. Setting periodic benchmarks that the sales team can celebrate can help maintain their motivation.

Techniques for Encouraging and Monitoring Team Development
Getting Sales Teams Excited

Acknowledgment and Prizes: These two factors are strong inducers of motivation for sales teams. Acknowledging and applauding accomplishments, no matter how little, can raise spirits and motivate ongoing work. Incentives might be in the form of cash, bonuses, praise from the public, or non-cash benefits like extended vacation time or unique rights.

Establishing a Competitive Landscape

Motivation and performance can be increased by fostering a positive competitive atmosphere. Salespeople can be motivated to push themselves to the limit and strive for perfection by using sales contests, leaderboards, and performance-based incentives. Making ensuring that competition doesn't turn a workplace into a nasty place to work is crucial.

Offering Ongoing Education and Training

Putting money into the ongoing education and training of the sales staff shows that you care about their success and development. Continuing professional development, product knowledge updates, and skill advancement opportunities are important ways to maintain salespeople's motivation and engagement. Sales teams with proper training are more assured and successful in reaching their objectives.

Clearly Outlining Expectations

An overwhelming sense of direction and purpose is given by well-defined expectations. Sales teams ought to be well-versed in their objectives, methods for reaching them, and standards of success. Maintaining focus and coordinating individual efforts with the overarching goals are made easier with regular feedback and communication.

Providing Assistance and Materials

It's critical to give sales teams the tools and resources they need in order for them to succeed. This covers administrative assistance, marketing materials, and technology and tool access. Providing salespeople with the resources they require for success can have a big impact on their motivation and productivity.

Monitoring Group Development

Frequent Evaluations of Performance

For the purpose of giving feedback and monitoring progress, regular performance reviews are crucial. These evaluations ought to determine areas for development, acknowledge accomplishments, and compare team and individual performance to predetermined targets.

Performance evaluations offer a chance for continual improvement and helpful criticism.

Dashboards and Reports for Sales

Real-time insights into sales success can be obtained through reporting tools and dashboards for sales. Sales managers can keep an eye on important indicators, monitor target progress, and spot patterns and trends with the help of these tools. Dashboards can offer a visual depiction of performance, which facilitates comprehension and outcomes communication.

Individual Consultations

Meetings one-on-one between team members and sales managers offer a forum for individualized support and feedback. In-depth talks regarding performance, difficulties, and development requirements are possible during these sessions. Frequent check-ins support upholding accountability and quickly resolving problems.

Collaborating and Holding Team Meetings

Frequent team meetings promote unity and cooperation. These gatherings offer a chance to talk on advancements, exchange perspectives, and come up with answers to problems. Innovative concepts and tactics for reaching sales targets might come from cooperative talks.

An overview of the main ideas

Any sales team's ability to set and meet specific targets is essential to their success. Having well-defined objectives is crucial since it helps with direction, performance evaluation, team building, and strategic planning. Using the SMART criteria, creating KPIs, and performing market research are some techniques for creating targets that are both reasonable and reachable.

Using performance tracking tools, constant training and development, incentives and rewards, and regular communication are some strategies for inspiring and monitoring team progress. Sales teams may maintain their motivation, attention, and alignment with the goals of the organization by putting these strategies into practice.

The Effects of Successful Sales Techniques on Business Development

The expansion of a corporation is significantly impacted by effective sales tactics. Increased revenue and market share result from targeted and effective sales efforts, which are ensured by well-defined strategy and goals. Sales teams that are driven and have received proper training are better able to establish trusting bonds with clients, encourage referrals, and succeed over the long haul.

Promotion of Continuous Learning and Adjustment in Sales

The environment of sales is always changing due to shifts in client preferences, market dynamics, and technology. Salespeople need to make a commitment to lifelong learning and adaptability if they want to remain competitive. Achieving consistent success in sales requires adopting new technologies, staying current on market trends, and making continuous improvements.

www.ingramcontent.com/pod-product-compliance
Lightning Source LLC
Chambersburg PA
CBHW071500220526
45472CB00003B/864